D0760645

MennoFolk

Studies in
Anabaptist and Mennonite History
No. 43

MennoFolk

Ervin Beck

Studies in
Anabaptist and Mennonite
History

Series Editor Steven M. Nolt; with Editors Gerald Biesecker-Mast, Geoffrey L. Dipple, Marlene G. Epp, Rachel Waltner Goossen, Leonard Gross, Thomas J. Meyers, John D. Roth, Theron F. Schlabach, and Astrid von Schlachta.

The series Studies in Anabaptist and Mennonite History is sponsored by the Mennonite Historical Society. Volumes have been published by Herald Press, Scottdale, Pennsylvania and Waterloo, Ontario unless otherwise noted.

31. *Tradition and Transition: Amish Mennonites and Old Order Amish, 1800-1900*
    By Paton Yoder, 1991
32. *John Smyth's Congregation: English Separatism, Mennonite Influence, and the Elect Nation*
    By James Robert Coggins, 1991
33. *The Lord's Supper in Anabaptism: A Study in the Christology of Balthasar Hubmaier, Pilgram Marpeck, and Dirk Philips*
    By John D. Rempel, 1993
34. *American Mennonites and the Great War, 1914-1918*
    By Gerlof D. Homan, 1994
35. *Keeping Salvation Ethical: Mennonite and Amish Atonement Theology in the Late Nineteenth Century*
    By J. Denny Weaver, 1997
36. *Andreas Ehrenpreis and Hutterite Faith and Practice*
    By Wes Harrison, 1997, copublished with Pandora Press Canada
37. *Mennonite and Nazi? Attitudes Among Mennonite Colonists in Latin America, 1933-1945*
    By John D. Thiesen, 1999, copublished with Pandora Press Canada
38. *Dancing with the Kobzar: Bluffton College and Mennonite Higher Education, 1899-1999*
    By Perry Bush, 2000, copublished with Pandora Press U.S., and Faith & Life Press
39. *The Earth Is the Lord's: A Narrative History of the Lancaster Mennonite Conference*
    By John Landis Ruth, 2001
40. *Writing Peace: The Unheard Voices of the Great War Mennonite Objectors*
    By Melanie Springer Mock, 2003, copublished with Cascadia Publishing House
41. *This Teaching I Present: Fraktur from the Skippack and Salford Mennonite Meetinghouse Schools, 1747-1836*
    By Mary Jane Lederach Hershey, 2003, published by Good Books
42. *Building on the Gospel Foundation: The Mennonites of Franklin County, Pennsylvania, and Washington County, Maryland, 1730–1970*
    By Edsel Burdge Jr. and Samuel L. Horst, 2004
43. *MennoFolk: Mennonite and Amish Folk Traditions*
    By Ervin Beck, 2004

MennoFolk

Mennonite and Amish Folk Traditions

Ervin Beck

Herald Press

Scottdale, Pennsylvania
Waterloo, Ontario

Library of Congress Cataloging-in-Publication Data
Beck, Ervin.
  MennoFolk: Mennonite and Amish folk traditions / Ervin Beck.
    p. cm. — (Studies in Anabaptist and Mennonite history; no. 43)
  Includes bibliographical references.
  ISBN 0-8361-9276-1 (pbk.: alk. paper)
  1. Mennonites—United States—Folklore. 2. United States—Folklore.
I. Title. II. Series.
  BX8116.B43 2004
  398'.088'2897—dc22
                                        2004007090

MENNOFOLK
Copyright © 2004 by Herald Press, Scottdale, Pa. 15683
Published simultaneously in Canada by Herald Press,
  Waterloo, Ont. N2L 6H7. All rights reserved
Library of Congress Catalog Card Number: 2004007090
International Standard Book Number: 0-8361-9276-1 (paperback)
                                    0-8361-9285-0 (hardcover)
Printed in the United States of America
Cover design by Ingrid Hess, adapted, with permission, from a cover
  design for *Mennonite Life*
Book design by Merrill R. Miller

10 09 08 07 06 05 04 10 9 8 7 6 5 4 3 2 1

To order or request information, please call
1-800-759-4447 (individuals); 1-800-245-7894 (trade).
Website: www.heraldpress.com

To the memory of Joel Edward Beck (1964-1973)
and Sarah Elizabeth Beck (1970-1985),
precious jewels.

Contents

Foreword

Students of history have been latecomers to the study of folklore. Preferring to write about structures of formal power or cutting edge ideas, academics often neglected folklore—the unrecorded, often orally transmitted stories, songs, and customs that animate much of human life, even in modern and text-centered societies.

As early as 1846, Englishman William J. Thoms coined the term folklore to describe songs and legends that predated the printed page or never earned the right to be enshrined in print. For the next century, folklore remained the preserve of linguists and musicologists eager to uncover the primitive roots of what they believed was a progressively evolving human culture. Only in the 1940s did American historian Richard M. Dorson (1916-1981) begin to consider the possibilities of folklore for understanding how people lived and thought over time. For Dorson, folklore was not about catching the last glimpses of a quickly fading past, but about the vital core of any living community. Significantly, Dorson proposed that folklore could be an especially fruitful line of inquiry for understanding American immigrant and ethnic minority groups, whose distance from the centers of cultural power often limited historians' abilities to recover the depth and detail of their daily lives.

Following such pioneering leads, a few non-Mennonite scholars of Pennsylvania German folklore such as Alfred F. Shoemaker and Don Yoder, explored connections between music, material culture, and the spiritual and intellectual worlds of Mennonite and Amish people. Meanwhile, "Russian" Mennonite storytellers and academics, including Doreen Klassen and Victor Carl Friesen, preserved and perpetuated Low German songs and proverbs.

Yet remarkably few Mennonites took folklore seriously. Perhaps their religious commitments led them to confuse fiction with the fictitious, unsure if truth could be found in jokes, legends, and tales. Perhaps the scholars among them saw folklore's focus on the unsophisticated and the ordinary as incompatible with their desire for professional respectability and community acceptance.

Fortunately, Ervin Beck, a native of the Pettisville, Ohio, Mennonite community and a long-time professor of English at Goshen College, was not content to ignore the oral, traditional, and mundane elements of Mennonite life. Quietly and carefully he was gathering origin tales, interpreting urban legends, collecting reverse painting on glass, and analyzing ethnic festivals. *MennoFolk: Mennonite and Amish Folk Traditions* brings together new and newly revisited folklore studies from Beck's years of research and consideration. His work is testimony not only to his scholarly care, but also to his devotion to the people whose cultural vitality he tapped. The results are a treasure for folklorists, but also for anyone who cares about the Mennonite experience, and especially for Mennonite historians concerned with questions of conduct, community, and conviction.

For a church whose understanding of faithfulness was expressed in daily choices and domestic routine, attention to folklore promises to yield insights into practical theology. Moreover, the orally and informally perpetuated aspects of folklife suggest new ways to understand the nature of community and the role of family in Mennonite and Amish history. And since folk culture is caught more than taught, it also illustrates the way in which Amish and Mennonites perpetuate tradition from generation to generation, illuminating a central task of religious people who must convince their children to continue in the faith.

The series Studies in Anabaptist and Mennonite History is pleased to offer *MennoFolk* as a contribution toward a deeper understanding of Mennonite peoplehood, past and present. Historians—and all who join the discussion of Mennonite life and faith—will only find their understanding enriched. May the conversation joined here, continue and flourish.

—*Steven M. Nolt, Series Editor*
Studies in Anabaptist and Mennonite History
Goshen College, Goshen, Indiana

Preface

After I coined the word *MennoFolk* for the title of this book, I discovered that it is also used by a group of Mennonite young people who have sponsored a summer music festival at Camp Friedenswald near Cassopolis, Michigan, and elsewhere in the U.S. and Canada. The newspaper article that announced the 2003 event emphasized "Mennonite-style singing with instrumentation styles from Cajun to Latin to Bluegrass to pop and Celtic." The Mennofolk website (www.mennofolk.org) says that this "volunteer-driven movement" honors "the integral influence of folk music in the Mennonite church."

My and their uses of the same word, *MennoFolk*, illustrate the complex and contradictory differences between the popular and the academic uses of the terms *folk* and *folklore*.

Mennofolk, the festival, clearly takes its inspiration from mainstream American culture, which reaches us through many commercialized channels of mass media—television, newspapers, films, recordings, websites. Folklorists regard such culture not as *folk culture* but as *popular culture*. And we further distinguish both of those spheres of culture from *academic culture*, which comes to us through authoritative channels—classrooms, textbooks, lectures, art galleries, concert halls.

In this scheme of things, *folk culture* is transmitted unselfconsciously through informal channels within a particular community.[1] Through "oral tradition and customary example," folklorists say. For verbal folk culture (stories, proverbs, songs), "oral tradition" refers to the traditional knowledge that we learn through word-of-mouth communication in small groups—usually in conversational settings, seldom in stage performances. We learn it "by ear" and "by heart." For material folk culture (art, gardens, costumes), "customary example" refers to what we learn by working next to a master and learning by imitation, often unselfconsciously so. In both verbal and material folk culture, the results are both predictable and creative, since the transmission will always be of "old" materials but with innovative elements.

A truly "Mennofolk" music program would consist of Old Order Amish singing their nearly 500-year-old hymns in their melismatic way. Or of Mennonites singing hymns and gospel songs in unaccompanied four-part harmony. Those are very distinctive folk musical traditions—surviving over many years, constantly evolving, and being passed on by customary example, rather than formal instruction or mass media.

If folklorists find little that is traditionally "Mennonite" in the music or the singing style or the stage performance in the Mennofolk music festival, they do see some elements of a latent, developing folk tradition.

First, the festival does invoke a community identity in claiming to be somehow "Mennonite," and folklore normally is associated with a certain community, whether the community is based on ethnicity, age, occupation, gender, or religion. Second, the event is called a "festival," which is a conventional folk expressive genre. If the festival is held often enough, and if Mennonites make up the performers and audience, it will eventually develop its own recognizable *folk traditions*, or predictable customs and patterns of behavior, which characterize folklore. Like the Mennonite relief sale discussed in chapter 9, if the festival succeeds in remaining relatively free from the control of churches and foundations, its official sponsors, it will become an expressive venue for the Mennonite young people— "the folk"—who keep it going.

MennoFolk, the book, intends to bring to the greater self-awareness of Mennonites and interested non-Mennonites some traditional materials and behaviors among North American Mennonites that (1) have been learned by word of mouth or customary example, (2) have been transmitted to succeeding generations of Mennonites, (3) illustrate both long-established materials and creative variants of them and (4) express feelings, ideas, and values that are important for the individuals who pass them on in informal performance venues and for the community that unselfconsciously sponsors them. The book also occasionally considers folklore *about* Mennonites and Amish that is perpetuated by other groups.

The book assumes and attempts to show that Mennonites constitute a distinctive *folk group*. Alan Dundes' bottom-line definition of the term is *"any group of people whatsoever* who share at least one common factor," since "a group formed for whatever reason will have *some* traditions which it calls its own."[2] For Mennonites, that common element is a religious faith that descends from European Anabaptists in the sixteenth century. Although Mennonites are now a worldwide community—with churches that are native to Latin America, Africa, India, Indonesia and elsewhere—that one factor of religious faith unites them and makes up the boundary that distinguishes them from other groups. If they could be known, the oral traditions and customary behaviors directly related to all national or linguistic groups' expressions of Anabaptist faith would constitute "international Mennonite folklore." It is too early in the worldwide spread of Mennonitism to know exactly what that folklore consists of, although perhaps it has been evident at past Mennonite World Conferences and will become further known through the Global Mennonite History Project.[3]

Of course, each national and linguistic group of Mennonites represents a different *cultural* embodiment of Anabaptism and therefore cultivates a distinctive local Mennonite folklore. Each of such groups probably also constitutes a separate *ethnic group* in their sociological context. What makes Mennonites an ethnic group will be discussed further in chapter 2. Suffice it to say here that the Swiss-German Mennonites with whom this book is mainly concerned are an ethnic group because, in addition to religious faith, their sense of group-ness includes a similar history, immigration experience, language and cultural institutions, among many other things. Swiss-German Mennonites inevitably express that shared experience through oral traditions and customary behaviors that distinguish their group from others. Mennonite folklore is seldom entirely original with the group, but if Mennonites borrow lore or customs from other groups, Mennonites adapt them for use in a culturally distinctive manner.

Except for this Preface and chapter 2, the essays in *MennoFolk* were previously published in various publications, from 1984-2004, which accounts for the varying styles and degrees of documentation. Together, the nine chapters do not constitute a comprehensive survey of the folk traditions found among Mennonites in North America. Indeed, such a book would be impossibly large and too ambitious for any one person to attempt. However, the scope of such a survey is hinted at by the Suggested Readings at the end of the book.

Most of the materials in the book represent Mennonite culture; fewer represent Amish culture; and a very few come from Hutterite culture. Except when otherwise noted, the Mennonite materials come from Mennonites of Swiss-German origin, and normally from the (Old) Mennonite Church rather than the General Conference Church (terms used prior to the merger of the two bodies as the Mennonite Church USA in 2002). Furthermore, most of the oral texts and all of the fieldwork in festival and art represent Mennonite and Amish culture in Elkhart and LaGrange counties in north-central Indiana, which is my home.

Even so restricted a scope of informants and materials, however, is too large for current folklore studies, which emphasize meanings that arise from individual folklore performance in small group contexts. Hence, any generalizations made here about Mennonite and Amish folklore are speculative, needing to be proven by more focused study.

The narrative texts have been edited to varying degrees for readability; the literal transcriptions of all of the items, including the contexts of their collection, have been deposited in the Ervin Beck files in the Mennonite Church USA Archives, Goshen, Indiana. I am grateful to all persons who contributed materials to the collection on which the first five chapters are based.

I moved into the study of folklore thanks to the Study-Service Trimester at Goshen College, when my wife Phyllis and I were faculty leaders for three units in Belize in the 1975-76 academic year. I became fascinated by the wonderful songs and tales still being transmitted orally in Belizean Creole culture. My fieldwork in Belize in 1975-76 and again in 1979 resulted in a large collection of materials and many publications, beginning with the essay "Telling the Tale in Belize" published in *The Journal of American Folklore*.[4] From Belize culture I moved to the study of current folk culture in Yorkshire, England—songs, legends, wedding, and calendar customs—thanks to a Lilly Faculty Open Fellowship that enabled me to spend a sabbatical year in fieldwork at the Centre for English Cultural Traditions and Language at the University of Sheffield.

My interest in Mennonite folk culture also began in Sheffield, England, when Alice and Willard Roth, old friends, visited us during their year in Birmingham. During supper Alice suddenly began telling—as historical fact—a Mennonite version of the elevator incident urban legend, involving Reggie Jackson. Since I had just recently participated in the first international legend conference at the University of Sheffield, I insisted that she re-tell the Reggie Jackson story into a tape recorder the next morning at breakfast. All of my subsequent studies of Mennonite folklore stem from that moment. One subject of enquiry tended to suggest another; I followed the linked chain with no intention of being comprehensive in my work.

Professional folklorists will see in *MennoFolk* a traditional approach to folklore studies, since it consists mainly of collections of texts analyzed in terms of the Mennonite communities that informally sponsor them. Since folklore—being oral (speech) and customary (action)—truly exists only in situations of actual performance, current folklorists emphasize "context" over "text" and study the lore in relation to the "context of situation" rather than the "context of culture," to use terms suggested by the anthropologist Bronislaw Malinowski.[5] Most of my analysis will be of texts in their context of culture, although the discussions of urban legend, protest songs, and folk arts also deal with more situated uses of folk materials.

Folklorists will also notice a relative lack of ideology and cultural theory in my analysis of folk materials. I have pursued my personal interests in the field in a way that seemed most fruitful, considering the materials and my audience. If these essays bring new materials and perspectives to the field of Mennonite studies, then my goal has been achieved. And if the analysis appears on a continuum somewhere between cultural journalism and folkloristics, then I am satisfied, since I intend to reach audiences of general readers and people interested in Mennonite and Amish studies.

As a folklorist I am especially indebted to Richard Bauman, now of Indiana University, who admitted me to his NEH seminar on Oral Narrative in the (hot) summer of 1980 at the University of Texas. He wouldn't have done it this way, but I hope he likes the book. At the University of Sheffield my mentor in folklore was John Widdowson, who has valiantly established respect for folklore as an academic study in England. In Sheffield I also learned much from Doc Rowe, now a freelance folklorist in England, and Paul Smith, now director of the folklore program at Memorial University in Newfoundland. United States folklorists Jan Brunvand, Barbara Allen, and Betty Belanus also encouraged me at important stages of my work.

In academic circles folklorists, like underdog Avis, need to "try harder," because of the "triviality factor" that some academics perceive in folklore studies. Academics are often fascinated by esoteric, elite culture and even distant exotic cultures, but uninterested in the everyday culture near at hand. True, the new field of cultural studies has dignified the study of mass-mediated, popular culture, but even that academic movement still neglects the study of folk culture.

I am pleased to have this opportunity to thank the colleagues of mine at Goshen College who always encouraged my academic interest in folklore and folklife, especially John Lapp, John Fisher, Dan Hess, John Roth, Todd Davis, and the late John Oyer. Rebecca Haarer, Don Walters, and Faye Peterson inspired my study of folk art. But my greatest support and encouragement have come from my wife Phyllis, who has cheerfully learned more than any normal person would want to know about folklore and local culture.

·1·

Stories and Functions

Some Mennonites feel uneasy about telling funny stories. Two experiences of my own will illustrate what I mean.

The pastor of the church in which I grew up once told us from the pulpit: "Some people ask me why I never smile. I'll tell you why I never smile. The Bible never tells us that Jesus laughed. It only tells us that Jesus wept."

A Beachy Amish minister was talking to my folklore students one day about the Amish way of life. I asked him whether he ever tells stories that don't come from his own experience or the Bible. An electric pause followed. He finally exclaimed: "I hope not! I hope I'd never do such a thing!"

I was pleased to see that neither man was consistent in his stated position. While working with my pastor on a pea-viner one summer, I discovered that he enjoyed joking as much as anyone else. And several minutes after his statement, the Beachy Amish minister told us two stories that he claimed were true, but that a folklorist would recognize as never having happened.

Of course, neither brother has his biblical evidence fully in mind. My pastor apparently missed the humor in the parables of Jesus, as well as the fact that Jesus was a welcome guest at the wedding at Cana. The Beachy Amish minister likewise ignored the fact that the parables that Jesus told never "really happened."

The parables are "true," however—not the way historical events are true, but the way fiction is true. As an African proverb puts it, "There is no story that is not true." This applies, also, to the funny stories that we tell. My purpose here is to help clarify some of the cultural meanings and values found in seemingly trivial—some would even say "frivolous"—narratives.

One good way to appreciate such stories is to take seriously the functions that they may serve in Mennonite culture, especially by following the insights of anthropologist William Bascom in his essay "The Four Functions of Folklore."[1] Although Bascom is concerned about all cultures and all forms of folklore—jokes, proverbs, riddles, recipes, games, festivals— what he says applies particularly well to storytelling.

His main point is that, although the immediate value of stories may be entertainment, their more important, long-term value is that they help maintain cultural stability. Although folklore may serve many functions in a culture, Bascom emphasized that folklore often validates culture, educates and controls people, and offers accepted means of rebelling against social controls.

I will summarize his points and illustrate them with examples from my collection of "Mennonite" stories, by which I mean stories told by Mennonites about themselves or related groups. Of course, a story may fit within more than one of Bascom's four categories, depending on how the story is interpreted or on the social context in which it is actually told.

Validation

Mennonites tell many stories that validate their peculiar culture. That is, they tell stories that help justify or explain why they do certain things or why they are a certain kind of people. Such stories often deal with the most peculiar traits of the culture. Frequently they reach back into the history of the clan to show where it all began.

One of the most interesting stories of this type is told about Menno Simons (1496-1561), the most articulate spokesman for Dutch Anabaptism:

Menno was preaching in a barn. And as was the custom, the women sat in the center and the men around the outside to protect them, as was typical of the churches in that day as well. And there was a shout outside that the sheriff had come to arrest Menno. So the men barred the way. Menno was standing on a molasses barrel for his pulpit and in his haste to get down, the end of the barrel caved in and he sank to his knees in molasses and would have laid a gooey track in escaping. So all the women in the front row each took one long lick of molasses off his hosen [leggings]. And that explains why Mennonite children in Holland to this day have a sweet tooth.[2]

A more likely reason for their sweet tooth may be that the early Dutch Mennonites grew wealthy through international trade in luxury goods, which enabled them to buy expensive things like sugar. But attributing it all to Menno gives their habit a quasi-religious sanction.

All of chapter 3 is devoted to discussing other similar etio-logical, or origin, accounts passed on by Mennonites, Amish,

and Hutterites. Along with many other topics, they explain the origin of the Mennonite Lie and the family names of Yoder and Warkentin, as well as why the Hutterites sing so loudly and why Amish women in northern Indiana face the wall when they stand to pray. Only two more origin accounts will be given here.

Here is one about why the Forks Mennonite Church near Middlebury, Indiana, still has clear-glass windows:

> This is a true story. It happened at Forks Mennonite Church. Lightning hit our church building and burned it down around 1940 or '38 or so. And in the process of rebuilding it the young people (I was one of them) were interested in having colored windows—stained-glass windows—put in the new church. And one brother made the statement, "Do you mean to say that you want to shut out God's sunlight?" And then another brother sitting there said, "It's very important to me to be able to sit here in church and see my farm buildings a half mile away." And about that time they took a vote and we lost the motion to have stained-glass windows in the church.

Finally, the origin of church splits is embodied in many stories, usually in versions that differ, depending on which side of the split is telling the story. One account, attributed to an Oregon Mennonite setting, could probably apply to all others:

> Apparently some years ago there was a division in one of the Oregon congregations. And a person asked, "Well, just what is it that keeps these two congregations in a state of feud most of the time?" And a member said, "Well, we really don't remember what it was, but we're not going to forget it!"

Education

Stories that validate culture are supported by stories that educate members of a culture. Indirectly, they teach young or new members how to act or think in order to be fully integrated into the culture and its values. These stories usually reflect the noblest goals of a culture and are often historically true, or at least claimed to be so.

One story about Menno proves to the believer that the Lord will come to the rescue in difficult situations:

> At another time this same traitor, in company with an officer or police, as they were in search of Menno, unexpectedly met him as he was going along on the canal, in a small boat. The traitor kept silent until Menno had bypassed them some distance, and had leaped ashore in order to escape with less peril. Then the traitor cried out, "Behold, the bird has escaped!" The officer chastised him—called him a villain, and demanded why he did not tell of it in time; to which the traitor replied, "I could not speak for my tongue was bound." The lords were so displeased at this that the traitor, according to his promise, had to forfeit his own head. It is worthy of consideration, how wonderfully God, in this and in other like instances preserves his people, and especially how fearfully he punishes the tyrants.[3]

This story is unusual since, along with their Mennonite descendants today, the early Anabaptists apparently told relatively few supernatural stories.

The Sermon on the Mount often gets restated in stories that teach Christian love at work in everyday affairs:

> I found in my father's papers sometime after he passed away this story about Alf Buzzard. They were having an all-day meeting. I think maybe it was one of these all-day Sunday school meetings. And one preacher was talking about the young people and how to discipline them—how to get them into the order of the church and cooperate. And he said, "It's just like the young colts. We must break them with bit and bridle—break them into submission." And after a while Alf Buzzard said, "We always found that it helped a lot to feed them sugar."

A third teaching story emphasizes that Mennonite fellow-ship is no longer limited to a northern European ethnicity:

> Two Mennonites from rural Virginia were in Chicago for an agricultural equipment seminar, so they called the pastor of one of the Mennonite churches for the location and time of Sunday worship. They accepted the pastor's invitation to spend Saturday night with them and attend worship on Sunday morning. After the worship experience in the former Presbyterian sanctuary with padded pews, with Mexican-American fellow worshipers singing songs in Spanish and not another plain coat in sight, they had a lot of questions. "Is this really a Mennonite church? We didn't know that there were Mennonites who spoke Spanish!" The following Wednesday evening during the Bible study at the Chicago church, one of the older Spanish ladies asked, "Those people who were in church on Sunday—were they Mennonites?"

More ethnic and religious instruction than we realize occurs by means of such stories, which remain in our memories after abstractions fade and admonitions grow wearisome.

Social control

Of course, not everyone is able at all times to meet the highest aspirations of the community. In cases of deviation from the norm, the community draws upon a body of stories that chasten and correct the erring member. Usually these stories are satirical. They correct by directing group laughter against the offending behavior. In my collection of Mennonite stories, this type by far outnumbers the other three types. Although this is probably true of all folk groups, it is appropriate to Mennonites, given their persistent problem in helping each other conform to their special beliefs and practices.

One story helps control Mennonites' proverbial passion for getting hard work finished early:

This was supposedly a line that my grandpa told somebody else. But he always prided himself on being the first one out into the field. And people just wondered, why so early sometimes? He'd be out at four o'clock and people just gave up trying to beat him—my dad—and his brothers out into the field. And finally somebody asked him once, "Why do you go out so early to the field?" "So we can quit early." "Well, why do you quit early?" "So we can have supper early." "Well, why do you have supper early?" "So we can get our chores done." "Well, why do you want to get your chores done early?" "So we can go to bed early." "Well, why do you go to bed early?" "So we can get up early in the morning."

An outsider's attempt to change Mennonite behavior generated the following story. Whether it will create more Democrats or Independents in Mennonite communities is debatable:

My grandfather used to tell me a story about a Democrat coming out and trying to get Mennonites to join the Democratic Party. And he came and gave his usual spiel to my grandfather, and my grandfather said, "No, I'm sorry, I'm not interested!" And the man said, "You know, there's 300 Mennonites here north of Doylestown from Blooming Glen over to Deep Run. And if the devil himself were on the Republican ticket, they'd vote for him!"

Prominent Mennonites in the fellowship attract many stories that expose their assumed weaknesses. Even popular, gentle S. C. Yoder, president of Goshen College from 1923 to 1940, is the object of satire:

I have another one on the bumbling hero. The version I heard was about S. C. Yoder, who made many trips. And on one occasion, when he was down at the train station, just before he got on the train, he called his wife to ask her where he was going. And she said, "Why don't you look at your ticket?"

This, of course, is an example of the "absent-minded professor" story type. Also told about Nelson Kauffman when he was director of the Mennonite Board of Missions and Charities, it is a good example of the many satirical stories that keep the great among us humble.

Compensation

Members of a close-knit group like the Mennonites, with distinctive beliefs and practices, must have some way to express hostile feelings when they feel oppressed by having to conform. One way of doing so is to tell stories whose contents are in blatant conflict with official group norms. Bascom says that such folklore enables people to "compensate" in a socially approved way for the oppression they feel. The stories serve as an "escape valve" for people to let off steam.

In this category belong all of the unprintable stories—blasphemous, heretical, obscene—that Mennonites tell about themselves. Most will remain unprinted here, too, because their proper context is not a public one—whether pulpit or book published by the denominational publishing house—where

offense would be great. Rather, their proper context is the intimate situation where the teller, who intends no offense, can tell a story to an audience that will likewise take no offense. Both teller and audience are comfortable because they know each other well enough to see that the words are emotionally therapeutic and not matched by willed or actual conduct. Such separation of statement from intention may be puzzling to Mennonites, who normally insist upon integrity of speech. The integrity of such stories lies in the fact that they observe the rules and expectations of fiction, not real life.

Some mildly compensatory stories in my collection suggest the nature and function of the stronger ones in this category. Most have to do with scandalous behavior by the presumed best among us, especially missionaries and college professors.

Mennonite missionaries in India didn't drink alcoholic beverages, but it was fun to imagine that they did:

> Four of our missionaries were away at a convention. This is a true story, too—at least, told to me for true out there. Anyway, they went to a missionary convention and they sent a wire home that they were coming back late at night. And among the four were Dr. Eash and Atlee Brunk. When the wire got home (and I'll substitute the first two names because I don't remember who they were) it came: "Hostetler Miller Each Drunk arriving on the midnight train."

Folklorists recognize in this irreverent tale yet another particularized version of the jumbled-telegram legend told by people in many countries.

Students also like to turn the tables on their superiors:

> A dean at Eastern Mennonite College was showing a guest around the campus. On the sidewalk they saw a cigarette butt and, ahead of them, a boy known to be a troublemaker. The dean picked up the butt and hurried forward to confront the student: "Who has been smoking on campus?"

The boy looked innocently at the cigarette butt and replied, "It must be a faculty member because students aren't allowed to smoke."

Finally, the naughtiest story fit to be printed here:

> A mother was giving some important instructions to her young daughter: "When the Lutheran preacher comes, hold on to Mommy's purse tight and don't let it go, no matter what. When the Salvation Army preacher comes, stand in front of the food pantry and don't move, no matter what. But when the Mennonite preacher comes, you crawl up on Mommy's lap and don't get off, no matter what!"

The editor of *Gospel Herald*—the former official periodical of the (Old) Mennonite Church, where this essay was first published—cut this story from the manuscript, claiming that the punch line was too obscure. Some years later, when many male Mennonite leaders were being accused of sexual harassment, the meaning of the story certainly became very clear, as well as less "compensatory" and more "satirical"—which illustrates that all of these stories can have more than one function and that those functions change, depending on historical and social contexts.

Conclusion

Many other functions could be added to Bascom's basic four. Alan Dundes, for instance, adds the general one of promoting "solidarity" among group members and the specific one of converting work into play, as with work songs.[4]

And Bascom's analysis can be criticized in two ways. First, Elliott Oring says that functional study has "explained nothing" about folklore, but merely helps point out the results of and "interrelations between cultural practices." The functions are descriptive analyses of cultural materials but constitute interpretation, or guesswork, rather than deep understanding of the nature of folklore.[5]

Second, Bascom's functionalism is too conservative a view of folklore's contribution to culture. All four functions, he concludes, contribute to stabilizing the culture that nourishes the folklore—by justifying the culture, by educating its members, by correcting them, and by offering a socially acceptable way for them to express their frustrations with the culture. True, folklore may contribute to cultural stability, but since all cultures change constantly, does folklore not also contribute to that change? Bascom's Freudian analysis of the fourth function—compensation—is the one most open to dispute. Culturally offensive stories, for instance, may also help change Mennonite culture in the direction of their logic, and not just offer moments of culturally harmless escape.

Mennonite culture, being essentially a conservative culture, may "need" Bascom's functions more than some other cultures today do. Folk narratives exert a conservative influence among us. Innovation enters the community most often through the mass media (popular culture) and avant garde thinking in the academic world (elite culture). Folklore maintains what has been good in the past. It derives its authority and stabilizing power from the relatively long history— "tradition," folklorists call it—that lies behind every item of folklore.

But Mennonite culture in the twenty-first century is much changed since World War II, and it continues to change rapidly. Folklore may slow that process, but perhaps some compensatory folklore also accompanies or even helps bring about such change, as with the Civilian Public Service (CPS) protest songs and certain aspects of Mennonite relief sales to be discussed in chapters 6 and 9, respectively.

Of course, it would be unwise to bring these understandings and questions to conscious awareness next time we tell or hear a story. That would spoil all the fun and probably also the social benefits. Instead, this analysis of function will serve Mennonites best by assuring them that the stories they tell probably do them more good than harm. Indeed, the Mennonite community has survived and prevails partly because of them.

·2·

Inter-Mennonite Ethnic Slurs

D o Mennonites constitute an ethnic group?

According to many thoughtful Mennonites today—especially mission-minded ones—Mennonites *should not* regard themselves as ethnics, lest cultural baggage interfere with the message of faith and hope that Mennonites have to offer to others.

Indeed, according to one authoritative source, *The Harvard Encyclopedia of Ethnic Groups,* Mennonites *are not* a distinct ethnic group. That encyclopedia offers separate entries for the Amish and the Hutterites, but it considers Mennonites under the general entry of "Pennsylvania Germans," not even naming Mennonites as such in that discussion.[1]

"Ethnicity" has always been a difficult term to define, and sometimes is a matter of intuition—or of feeling "ethnic"— rather than of formulaic analysis. Especially for immigrant groups in the U.S., ethnicity derives from some kind of mix of common geographic origin, history of immigration, racial stock, religious faith, settlement and employment patterns, political interests, institutions, native language, and distinctive foods, costumes, literature, music, folklore, etc. All of which Swiss-German Mennonites, for instance, share. In addition, people who *think* they are ethnically distinctive, or people whom others *regard* as ethnically distinctive, are probably ethnics in reality. And Mennonites and Amish certainly think that they are different from other people—at least at certain times and in certain ways.

Even if we had no other evidence of Mennonite ethnicity, the ethnic slurs that Mennonites nurture in their oral traditions, or folklore, show that Mennonites have a keen, if intuitive, sense of belonging to an ethnic group, and that they experience a kind of rivalry with other ethnic groups, even other Mennonite ethnic groups.

Ethnic slurs are words, sayings, stories, and jokes that, on the surface at least, tend to elevate one ethnic group (usually that of the teller) at the expense of the ethnic group that is the butt of the joke or joking comment. Although educated Mennonites will condemn and abjure the use of ethnic slurs against other groups in American and Canadian culture—Jews, African-Americans, Newfoundlanders, Polish—they seem to have no qualms about perpetuating and enjoying ethnic slurs against related Anabaptist groups—and also against their own group.

The existence of this body of ethnic slurs suggests that Mennonites are a distinctive ethnic group, since ethnic slurs always indicate that tellers and audience have a sense of the "boundaries" that separate and distinguish their ethnic group from another.

Ethnic slurs are the "sociology" of folk culture, since they communicate one group's general understandings of the distinguishing characteristics of their own group as opposed to those of the target group. These generalizations—or stereotypes—are based on communal experience and tradition, not empirical evidence, although sometimes stereotypes are amazingly accurate mirrors of some details of group behavior and self-perception.

This chapter will present jokes and funny stories about Mennonite groups and offer minimal interpretive comments on what each item implies. But what follows needs some important qualifications.

I collected almost all of the items in (Old) Mennonite Church contexts, such as Sunday school class storytelling sessions, and from Mennonite publications. Hence, my assumptions about which group tells the story or about which group is the target of the story are speculative and tentative, and therefore any conclusions about meanings or implications are suggestive rather than definitive.

The meaning, or effect, of telling any one of the joking items that follow depends entirely on the social context in which the telling takes place. Obviously, the negative impact of telling an ethnic or racist joke is less when a member of the target group tells it to his fellows (e.g., a Jew telling a Jewish joke to a fellow Jew) than when an outsider to the group tells it in the presence of a member of the target group (e.g., a gentile telling a Jewish joke with a Jew present). In fact, all of the items in this chapter are probably told more often in Mennonite in-group contexts than they are told in public contexts. Just as Jews probably know and use more jokes about Jews than other groups do, so do Mennonites know and use Mennonite jokes more often than other groups do.

Following each item I put in italics the stereotypical ideas about the group that the item seems to contain. However, in order for it to be understood properly and fully, each item really deserves to be considered in its complex historical, sociological, and psychological context whenever it is transmitted in "real life."

In labeling the groups of stories, I borrow terms from folklorist William Hugh Jansen, who uses *esoteric* to refer to lore that groups use about themselves and *exoteric* to refer to lore that groups use about other groups.[2]

I. Esoteric Mennonite jokes: What Mennonites think of themselves

The first story certainly puts Mennonites in a good light. In fact, this is the story that John L. Ruth, Mennonite historian, told me when I asked him what he regarded as the quintessential Mennonite story. It is wry, rather than funny, but it has a punch line characteristic of joking stories. The fact that it is serious rather than funny suggests the special assent that Mennonite tellers give to its representation of their group.

A.1: A Mennonite was standing on the street in Lancaster, Pennsylvania, one day when an evangelist came up to him and asked, "Are you saved, brother?" The Mennonite did not respond verbally. Instead, he got out some paper and a pencil from his pocket, wrote some things on it, and handed it to the street evangelist. "There," he said, "are the names and addresses of my wife, a man I do business with, and my next door neighbor. Ask them if I'm saved. I could tell you anything." *Mennonites eschew overt evangelism. They live out their faith, rather than giving verbal testimonies about it.* The story is also told, appropriately, about members of the Church of the Brethren.[3]

A.2: A group of Mennonites held a conference in a hotel in Chicago. And the bellhops started talking to each other and one said that the Mennonites were coming. The other asked, "Well, who are the Mennonites?" "Well," he said, "you'll know them. They've got the Ten Commandments in one hand, a ten-dollar bill in the other, and they leave without breaking either one." *Mennonites are provincial and don't know how to behave in the city. They do not compromise their moral principles when away from home. They are frugal, even stingy.* This joke overtly defines "Mennonite" and, like the preceding story, does so by citing what they do rather than what they say about themselves. This joke began circulating when Mennonites began holding meetings in urban conference centers, rather than in Mennonite communities. It often circulates following a major Mennonite conference.

A.3: A Catholic priest, a Jewish rabbi and a Mennonite preacher were all playing an illegal game of poker together in a dark back room. And the police came, and they quickly hid everything. And the police asked the Catholic, "Were you playing cards in here tonight?" The Catholic said, "Oh, no. No, I wasn't. I wasn't." The police asked the Jewish rabbi, "Were you playing cards?" "No. No, I wasn't." They asked the Mennonite. The Mennonite said, "With who?" *Even in the most compromising (and unlikely) situation, a Mennonite can, technically, preserve moral innocence and integrity of speech—making "yea be yea," which has always been a distinctive Mennonite principle.* Although this joke can be and is told about various religious persons, it fits perfectly within the "Mennonite lie" stereotype discussed in chapter 4.

While it is likely that A.2 and A.3 are told about Mennonites by non-Mennonites, most Mennonites would regard the stereotypes implied by those stories as representing positive attributes of their culture.

II. Exoteric Mennonite jokes: What non-Mennonites think about Mennonites

Since the following items give an overall negative view of Mennonites, they can represent non-Mennonites' ethnic slurs against Mennonites. The first item, a riddle joke, is clearly the Mennonite slur that non-Mennonites in northern Indiana are most likely to know and use, even in direct conversation with Mennonites. Oddly, it is probably also the Mennonite slur most known and used by Mennonites themselves.

B.1: Q: Why does Elkhart, Indiana, have all the blacks and Goshen, Indiana, all the Mennonites?

A: Because Elkhart had first choice.[4] *Mennonites are even more socially contemptible than African-Americans.* Goshen is the county seat of Elkhart County, but Elkhart is the larger city. Mennonites actually lived in Elkhart quite a while before they lived in Goshen. Elkhart became a railroad and industrial center, attracting an African-American community, while Goshen, until recent years, had virtually no African-American population. The fact that the joke can be freely told both inside and outside Mennonite circles suggests that its point is not true. Since the humor thrives on the culturally ingrained negative view of African-Americans, the joke is racist.

B.2: St. Peter was leading some new arrivals on a tour of heaven. After being shown around for a while they arrive at a room where St. Peter said, "You may have a free rein in heaven, except for this place, where you may not enter." "Why not?" asked the new saints. St. Peter whispered, "Because that's where the Mennonites are, and they think they are the only ones here." *Mennonites are spiritually arrogant and naïve in thinking that they alone will be saved. Their separatist stance encourages social standoffishness.*

B.3: A Presbyterian asked a Mennonite farmer, "According to your religion, if you had a hundred sheep, would you give me fifty?" "Certainly, I'd give you fifty," said the Mennonite. "If you had fifty horses, would you give me twenty-five?" "I certainly would." "And if you had two cows, would you give me one?" "That's not fair! You know I have two cows!" *As nonresistant Christians, Mennonites follow the "law of love," but only in hypothetical situations. In reality, they are selfish.* This story cuts to the heart of many Mennonites' self-perception.

B.4: Some Mennonite ministers were holding a meeting at a Holiday Inn, where a group of business executives were also meeting. The groups ate in banquet rooms adjacent to each other. The Mennonites ordered a typical Mennonite meal of chicken, mashed potatoes, etc. The businessmen ordered T-bone steaks, etc. Both groups ordered watermelon slices for dessert. The main courses were served as ordered, but when the busi-

nessmen ate their watermelon, they found that it was *not* soaked in brandy as they had ordered. When the waiter went to the Mennonites' room, he saw that the orders had become confused. The Mennonite ministers were smacking their lips and putting watermelon seeds in their shirt pockets. *Mennonites are frugal and enterprising. They are naïve in worldly matters. Their position of abstinence is hypothetical, not grounded in experience. They will succumb to alcohol like everyone else, given the opportunity, especially in a more urbanized culture.*

III. Exoteric Mennonite jokes: What (Old) Mennonites think of more conservative Anabaptist groups (Old Order Amish, Beachy Amish, Conservative Mennonites)

The ethnic slurs in the remainder of the chapter take for granted an understanding of the continuum from conservative to liberal that exists in Mennonite-related groups. The six Mennonite subgroups listed here merely represent those groups that appear in the Mennonite stories I have collected in northern Indiana. In actuality, there are at least thirteen different Amish groups and fifty-seven different Mennonite groups in the U.S. today.[5] Presumably, with study, one could find ethnic jokes referring to all of these groups in their neighbors' lore.

In the year 2002 the Mennonite Church and the General Conference Mennonite Church merged, creating Mennonite Church USA and Mennonite Church Canada. However, the earlier groupings are still evident to members of the new church:

General Conference Mennonite Church: most liberal theology and practice.

Mennonite Brethren Church: conservative theology, liberal practice.

(Old) Mennonite Church: liberal theology, conservative practice.

Conservative Mennonite Conference: conservative theology and practice.

Amish-Mennonite Church (Beachy Amish): liberal Amish theology and practice.

Old Order Amish: most conservative theology and practice. The jokes that follow will reveal certain ingrained subgroup rivalries, no doubt based on the history of church divisions and the fact that the subsequent rival groups continue to live in close proximity to each other. For instance, the General Conference Church split from American (Old) Mennonite and Amish Mennonite churches in 1860, becoming the more liberal denomination. This historic rivalry was presumably put to rest by the merger of the two churches in 2002. The rivalry between the General Conference Mennonite Church and the Mennonite Brethren Church has its origins in Russia in 1860, when the Mennonite Brethren split from other Mennonite colonists, wanting a more fervent, evangelical faith. When they immigrated, most Russian Mennonites joined the General Conference Mennonite Church in the U.S. and Canada, but the Mennonite Brethren retained their identity in North America and have continued to be geographic neighbors of their General Conference relatives.

The (Old) Mennonite and Amish rivalry stems from the 1690s, when the Amish, led by Jacob Reist and others, separated from the Mennonites in Switzerland, supporting the excommunication of members in enforcing church discipline. The Conservative Mennonite Conference separated from other Mennonite churches, beginning in 1910, wanting a more conservative application of scripture than the Mennonites, but a more active church program than the Old Order Amish. The Beachy Amish are known by various names throughout the U.S., including Amish-Mennonite. These congregations began splitting from the Old Order Amish in 1927, in order to use cars and other modern technology and to establish Sunday schools and mission programs.[6]

Members of the (Old) Mennonite Church in northern Indiana tell the most stories about their Old Order Amish cousins. So do non-Mennonites. One general reason is that the Amish have inherited the status earlier given to the stereotypical "Dumb Dutchman" in U.S. ethnic humor. Since the Amish (along with Old Order Mennonites) retain German as their native tongue, they remain the brunt of ethnic joking in German culture areas.

Perhaps Mennonites in Northern Indiana tell so many negative jokes about the Amish because Mennonites are otherwise so closely identified with Amish by non-Mennonites. If that is the case, then the jokes serve Mennonite culture by distancing Mennonite narrators from the backward Amish who threaten the social reputations of Mennonites. On the other hand, when it serves their purpose—namely when positive perceptions of Amish are being given attention—Mennonites can also tell jokes that reflect positively on Amish and thereby claim those positive values for themselves.

C.1: Two Amishmen were operating their snowmobile on Fish Lake [in eastern Elkhart County] when the ice broke and the snowmobile sank in the water. One Amishman dived into the water to retrieve it, but couldn't. His friend stayed on the ice, yelling down to him: "Choke it! Choke it!" *Amish, who drive horse and buggies rather than cars, are morons when it comes to technology.* In actual fact, they are very clever with small engine technology. Here their role as moron in German culture overwhelms their well-known mechanical abilities.

C.2: Long ago when airplanes were a novelty, two Amish men east of Goshen were watching a two-engine plane approach. The Amish man from Honeyville [LaGrange County] said, "Oh, he must be from Clinton Township [Elkhart County]. The plane has rubber tires." The Amish man from Clinton Township said, "Oh, no! I'm sure he's from Honeyville. He's smoking." *The Amish enforce trivial restrictions. The Amish are contradictory, varying in their discipline from group to group.* Amish districts in Elkhart County permitted hard rubber on their buggy wheels but forbade the use of tobacco, whereas Amish in LaGrange County eschewed rubber on buggy wheels but allowed smoking.

C.3: An Amish couple went to buy a farm. In the middle of the transaction, they discovered they didn't have enough money. The husband turned and scolded his wife: "Mom, you brought the wrong cream can." *The Amish are frugal and therefore very wealthy. They shun the banking system and use cash only. They even pay big bills in cash. Amish women live in a patriarchal culture.* Traditionally, Amish have been land-rich but cash-poor. Today they are more likely to have bank accounts.

C.4: An Amish woman gave birth to her fifteenth child in the hospital, rather than at home where she had had all of the others. She liked hospital delivery so much that she told all her friends, "I'm going to have all the rest of my babies in the hospital." *The Amish have extraordinarily large families. They love modern conveniences when they are acquainted with them. The Amish have a lot of sex, despite their puritanical appearance.* Mildly obscene stories about Old Order Amish abound. Today the Amish increasingly use community hospitals, as well as special Amish birthing clinics in their neighborhoods.

C.5: Q: How did they know that the newborn baby abandoned on the freeway was Amish?

A: Because it had a hook and eye rather than a bellybutton. *In certain costumes Amish must use hooks and eyes rather than buttons. The Amish are so odd that even their anatomy is different.* Amish buggies, of course, do not travel on freeways.

Q: What did the Polack do to his car when he joined the Beachy Amish Church?

A: He painted the windshield black. *Beachy Amish used to have to paint the chrome on their cars black as a sign of modesty and to avoid a flashy appearance.* Such a compromise was accepted by these liberalizing Amish in moving from horse and buggy to automobile transportation. The Beachy Amish are still sometimes called Black-Bumper Amish by their neighbors.

Q: What would you get if you crossed a Japanese and an Amish man?

A: A Toyoder. *One of the most widespread Amish family names is Yoder. The Old Order Amish seldom marry outside their ethnic group, and certainly not in cross-racial marriages.* However, they occasionally adopt children of other racial identities. Q: What did the Japanese Amish man do on December 7, 1941? A: He attacked Pearl Bontrager. *Pearl is a common, old-fashioned name for an Amish girl. Bontrager is, like Yoder, a very common Amish family name. Despite their modest clothing, the Amish are over-sexed.* As nonresistant Christians, the Amish would not participate in a military attack. The humor in this and the preceding joke derives from unexpected puns on Amish names. The linking by these two jokes of Amish with Japanese may be related somehow to the fact that there used to be a group of Japanese Hutterites in Japan who dressed like the Hutterites of North America.

The four items above are all riddle jokes—like the earlier one about Elkhart and the blacks. Whereas probably all joking *stories* could just as effectively be told about other ethnic groups, these *riddle jokes* remain bound to their ethnic references and are not transferable to other ethnic groups. It is easy to elaborate upon stories, changing their details. But the riddle joke is bound by such a short, rigid question and answer form that it is hard to change or elaborate upon, especially when puns are involved. In addition, all of these riddle jokes deal with very particular and peculiar idiosyncrasies of Amish groups— whether family names, black car bumpers, or hooks and eyes.

C.6: A Conservative Mennonite boy became engaged to an Old Order Amish girl. Someone asked him if they had decided which church to join, the Amish or the Conservative Mennonite Church. "Neither," he said. "We've decided to go all the way. We're going to join the Mennonite Church." *All of the more conservative Mennonite groups actually aspire to be liberal Mennonites.*

C.7: An Old Order Amish woman was lamenting that her daughter was engaged to marry a Conservative Mennonite boy. She exclaimed to her friend, "My daughter's turning liberal and joining the Conservatives." *Degrees of being "liberal" or "conservative" are ridiculous among the groups more conservative than the Mennonite Church.*

IV. Exoteric Mennonite jokes: What some Mennonite groups (Amish, Conservative Mennonites, General Conference, Mennonite Brethren) think about other Anabaptist groups

A Conservative Mennonite man told me the following story about an Amish man. Often reverting to Pennsylvania Dutch, the narrator could barely tell me the story in English, which suggests that it is an ethnic slur deeply ingrained in his culture.

D.1: During hard times a neighbor called upon his Amish friends next door. "My husband is in the back porch," the wife told him. On the back porch he saw his Amish neighbor fishing, with his line and hook in a bucket of water. "Why are you fishing in a bucket?" he asked. "I wouldn't be fishing in a bucket if I didn't need the fish so bad," the Amish man replied. *Amish man as moron again*—but in a strangely Zen-like story.

In my collection, the Amish are the butt of the joke more often than any other group. What ethnic slurs do the Amish use against their Anabaptist cousins? Oddly, I have been unable to find any such stories from the Amish community, despite asking my Amish and formerly Amish friends for examples. In fact, David Luthy, Amish librarian and publisher in Aylmer, Ontario, says that I will likely find no ethnic slurs against Mennonites in Amish culture. According to Luthy, Amish tell stories on themselves, but not about other groups.

For a folklorist, that is very hard to believe, since the Amish have such a boundaried community, threatened on all sides by the allure of more liberal Amish and Mennonite groups, that one would normally expect them to have an arsenal of such stories. Until some come my way, I will need to let stand Luthy's claim about the slur-defenselessness of the Old Order Amish.

Supporting Luthy's claim that Amish tell jokes on themselves but not on others, I will cite two riddle jokes that the

Amish near Goshen are known to tell on themselves:

D.2: Q: In a room full of Amish people, how do you get everyone's attention?

A: Say, "We are going to Wal-Mart."

Q: If eighty percent of the world were Amish, what would the other twenty percent be?

A: Van drivers. *The frugal Amish love to shop for bargains. The Amish compromise their principles by depending on more worldly people to get around.* Both contradict the Amish values of simplicity, of anti-materialism and of separation from the world.

In place of an Amish slur against another Anabaptist group, I merely offer a joking comment reportedly made by one Amish woman after she had listened to this moron story about her own people:

D.3: A tourist visiting Shipshewana, Indiana, was so impressed by the Amish faith that he decided he wanted to become Amish, too. So he went to his doctor and asked how he could be made into an Amish man. The doctor said it was possible, but very, very difficult and risky. "I will have to remove

part of your brain," he said. The man decided to risk the operation. Following the long, difficult ordeal, the surgeon hovered over his patient's bed, waiting to hear the first words he would utter. When he heard the patient say, "Wie gehts?" [Pennsylvania Dutch greeting] he knew the operation had been a success.

To which story an Amish woman, listening, added: "Yes, and then the dummy went and joined the Beachys!" [Beachy Amish Church]. *Her comment suggests that the Beachy Amish are moronic and the most threatening group for the Old Order Amish in northern Indiana.*

From the opposite end of the conservative-liberal spectrum come two slurs used by General Conference Mennonites (GC) against their main rivals, the more conservative (Old) Mennonite Church (OM).

D.4: A little girl was tending some newborn kittens along South Eighth Street in Goshen [site of a General Conference church] when a passerby asked her, "What kind of kittens are those?" She replied, "They're OM kittens." Two weeks later the same passerby saw her at the same place with the same kittens. He asked again, "What kind of kittens are those?" She replied, "They're GC kittens." Puzzled, he asked, "Two weeks ago you told me they were OM kittens. Why do you say they are GC kittens today?" She said, "Their eyes are open now." *The (Old) Mennonite Church is unenlightened.*

D.5: Q: What's the difference between the General Conference Mennonite Church and the (Old) Mennonite Church?

A: Twenty years. *OMs suffer a cultural lag of a full generation in "catching up" with the correct, more liberal stance of the GCs.* What Mennonite could argue with that analysis?

Here's a slurring joke-like version of what is claimed to have been an actual event, as seen by General Conference people in Henderson, Nebraska, at the expense of their Mennonite Brethren neighbors:

D.6: One weekend in Henderson, Nebraska, the large

General Conference Mennonite Church was holding a health fair for senior citizens, and the large Mennonite Brethren Church at the opposite end of town was holding a conference. A Mennonite Brethren man from Minnesota, who was unfamiliar with Henderson, entered town, looking for the MB church. Seeing a crowd at the GC church, he thought he was at the right place and joined a long line, assuming it was for registration. He waited and waited until he finally got to the table, only to be surprised and dismayed when the woman in charge gave him a paper cup and asked for a urine sample. "What kind of church is this?" he exclaimed. *MB's are pious morons. GC's are socially conscious activists.* Although natives of Henderson insist that the incident "really happened," the shaping of the story with a punch line suggests that it has become to some degree fictionalized. Some re-tellings say that the man came to Henderson for a missions conference, which enhances the stereotype that *Mennonite Brethren are more interested in evangelizing than in social justice.*

Finally, for good measure, one inter-Mennonite slur also glances satirically at a rival church in Canada. To get the joke, one must know that the Mennonite Brethren Church immerses new believers; the (Old) Mennonite Church baptizes theirs by pouring; and the United Church of Canada baptizes by sprinkling.

D.7: One summer it was so hot in Canada that the Mennonite Brethren resorted to baptizing their new members by pouring; the Mennonite Church, by sprinkling; and the United Church of Canada, by sending their candidates for baptism to the dry cleaners. *Doctrinal disputes about the correct manner of baptism are ridiculous. The United Church of Canada is over-refined.*

V. Mennonites and ethnic slurs

This abundance of ethnic slurs suggests that Mennonites have a keen sense of being a distinctive ethnic group and that they feel a need to distinguish themselves from other Mennonite groups by telling joking stories about themselves and others. In fact, the repertoire of Mennonite ethnic slurs is almost infinitely expandable, since many other stories, especially moron stories, can be adapted to inter-ethnic verbal combat.

But why do Mennonites, who have nurtured a tradition of truthful speech since their earliest origins, and who nowadays are so "politically correct," have no qualms about telling such stories, even in public situations? Possible answers to that question derive from the general nature of ethnic slurs and perhaps also from the nature of the Anabaptist community.

Folklorists who study ethnic slurs notice that they are not the lethal social weapons that they appear to be when considered outside contexts of actual use. Ethnic slurs are conventionalized, formalized aesthetic items. They are different from the calculated insults that a vicious person might compose in hateful speech toward another person or group. The performer of an ethnic slur reaches for an already formed expression—a kind of proverb—for which his community, not he himself, is accountable. And the sting is usually relieved by humor.

Also, the slur is usually delivered in casual conversation in private meetings of intimate friends. The performer intends no harm and the audience perceives no harm in it. In such a situation the slur works to reinforce group solidarity among teller and audience, probably more so than it negatively affects the target group.

If otherwise politically correct Mennonites tell inter-Mennonite ethnic slurs with abandon, that may indicate that members of Mennonite-Anabaptist groups see themselves, more or less, as belonging to one single family of believers, more or less. Inter-Mennonite ethnic jokes therefore resemble the teasing that regularly occurs among members of a nuclear family. The nagging exception to this perhaps panglossian idea are the many harsh jokes that Mennonites tell about the Old Order Amish and Old Order Mennonites. That thoughtlessness may be implicitly encouraged by the tendency of old order groups to separate themselves from Mennonites and other groups, and to not defend themselves when offended.

Wishes aside, ethnic slurs are not likely to disappear from human interaction, despite widespread condemnation of them today. They may recede even more from the sphere of public discourse, but they will always have a welcome home, somewhere, among members of groups that perceive themselves as different from other groups.[7]

Origin Tales and Beliefs

E tiological tales and beliefs are traditional stories and notions
that explain the origin or cause of things that are part of
everyday experience but nevertheless have something bizarre or
anomalous about them.[1] Passed on by word of mouth, usually
over many generations, these explanations may or may not be
historically verifiable—they usually are not—but because they
persist in the popular belief-systems of communities, their
importance exceeds the mere question of whether or not they
are factually true.

We tend to associate such traditional wisdom only with the
folklore of exotic cultures, and find their explanations charming
and exotic rather than personally compelling. For instance,
among the Uncle Remus stories of African-American culture is
one that explains why Brer Wasp cannot laugh. Likewise, one
story about the spider Anansi in African-Caribbean lore
explains why there are fools in the world today.[2] And a Paiute
tale of the hero Coyote explains why Bobcat and Coyote are
eternal enemies.[3]

These animal stories from primitive cultures feature trickster heroes who, scholars think, may originally have been creation deities for the cultures that transmit their stories.[4]
Although we may find it hard to take such explanations seriously, they are key documents for understanding the basic values of their cultures.

Closer home, we do take seriously the etiological stories

from the Christian tradition that are, in their own ways, as colorful as the trickster tales from African and Native American cultures. The book of Genesis ("birth") contains most of these, the most striking of which are the accounts of the creation of the world, the creation of humankind, the origin of evil, the origin of many languages, and the origin of the rainbow. Both Christians who regard the stories as literal accounts and others who see them as figurative find indispensable, ultimate truths embodied in them.

We are less likely to notice—let alone interpret—the etiological beliefs and tales that arise from our own folk communities. Although all human groups nurture origin accounts, Mennonite-related groups may perpetuate them more than other groups do. At least insofar as Mennonites are a separate, peculiar people with peculiar customs and a peculiar history, they might logically be expected to transmit more etiological accounts than most Americans, simply because they need more help in "explaining"—and thereby vindicating—their otherwise anomalous customs and beliefs.

As we shall see, Mennonite etiological accounts range from the ridiculous to the sublime—that is, from jokes to the conclusions of academic scholarship. Whether jokes or judgments, however, all serve a vital role in creating and stabilizing the identities of the groups that perpetuate them.

Four relevant qualifications are in order. First, these Mennonite etiological accounts emerged during my collection of other kinds of Mennonite folklore. They are not the product of exhaustive search. They constitute a tentative survey of what might be found in greater abundance if Mennonite, Amish and Hutterite traditions were collected and analyzed more thoroughly. Second, I mix Mennonite, Amish, and Hutterite items because I assume that a core of beliefs and experiences unites these people. Of course, the ideal would be to have enough beliefs and stories from each group to make possible separate studies of the special experience of each group. Third, sometimes I have not collected enough versions of each item to document conclusively that it is traditional lore, although I am persuaded by the items and the context of their collection that all are indeed traditional.

Finally, I have set up the etiological accounts in question-and-answer form, even though they almost never appear in real life in such a self-consciously explanatory structure. Usually they appear in conversational contexts as cryptic legends or shorthand, proverb-like segments of belief that supply a context for other topics being discussed. Although origin accounts normally appear in folklore studies as straightforward declarations, I use the dialectic form here to stress the questioning impulse that is basic to the genre and also to unify, in printed format, the varied kinds of materials—jokes, legends, beliefs, scholarly conclusions—used in this study.

Exoteric Etiological Accounts[5]

The nature of the genre may be most easily perceived by first examining origin beliefs held about Mennonites by people from other groups. This is *exoteric* lore, to use William Hugh Jansen's term, since it is lore about Mennonites perpetuated by outsiders.[6] The misunderstandings in these exoteric origin accounts are so blatantly in error that they prepare the otherwise credulous reader to be more skeptical about items later in the essay that seem more plausible but that are no less open to rational challenge.

Q. *Why do Amish paint their front gates blue?*

A. To indicate that there is a girl of marriageable age in the family.[7]

Q. *Why do Mennonites leave their barn doors open on Sunday?*

A. The interview with the State Arts Commission had gone well. The questions had been routine until Claudia Bowen leaned forward and said, "I have a different question altogether. Do you mind?" "Of course not," I replied. "I notice that you are a Mennonite," she began. "I was told by Celia Schultz, a former Mennonite from Illinois who founded the Seattle Opera

Company, that when a Mennonite farmer had a daughter that was eligible for marriage, they would leave the barn door open on Sundays so that the young men would see it and drop by, after church, offer to close the door and meet the young girl. Now the question I want to ask is: 'If that is what they do on the farm to marry off their daughters, what do the Mennonites do when they live in the city?'"[8]

Amish and Mennonite insiders know that these explanations err because the questions themselves are based on false understandings. The Amish, as a group, do not paint their front gates blue, and Mennonites do not intentionally leave their barn doors open on Sunday.

True, in interior decoration Amish have in the past often used light blue paint—sometimes called "Amish blue" by outsiders. Their infrequent use of blue outdoors in an otherwise stark white decor may be odd enough to inspire beliefs like this one.

The barn door belief may spring from the reputation that Mennonites have for being hard-working, meticulous caretakers of their farmsteads. How, then, to explain a barn door left open on a Sunday? If carelessness must be ruled out because Mennonites are such careful farmers, then an explanation suggesting purposeful conduct must be supplied. Hence, the notion about advertising for marriage.

The images in these beliefs encourage a deeper Freudian speculation. If gate and door suggest the vagina awaiting penetration, then the questions thinly disguise outsiders' concerns about Mennonite and Amish intercourse, rather than quaint courtship customs. In collecting Mennonite and Amish stories I have been impressed by the great number of jokes that outsiders tell regarding sex among these people, especially the Amish. Most such jokes are unprintable in Mennonite publications. These bawdy stories may spring from outsiders' fixation with, on the one hand, the large families traditionally found in these groups and, on the other, the sexless messages that the costumes and demeanor of the "plain people" express in public. "How do Amish and Mennonites mate?" is a reasonable response by outsiders, and their traditional explanations, correct or not, satisfy part of their curiosity.

Q. *Why do the Indiana Amish have weddings on both Thursday and Sunday, and more weddings on Thursday than on Sunday?*

A. Couples who get carried away while bundling must marry on Thursday. Only the few couples who exercise sexual restraint are allowed to marry on Sunday.[9]

While it is true that Amish weddings are held on both days, and more on Thursday than Sunday, few Amish practice bundling anymore.[10] Almost the only couples who have Sunday weddings are older people, especially those entering second marriages, for whom the kind of full-day celebration held for young couples on Thursday would not be appropriate.

Why do the Amish hold weddings on Thursday? The best answer may be that they have always done so. According to William I. Schreiber, having weddings on Thursday (and Tuesday) is an ancient custom that predates even the Christian era.[11] In practical terms for modern Amish culture, having weddings on Thursday rather than Sunday helps break up the long work week for Amish farmers and laborers and also allows time for the Amish host families (including newlyweds) to clean up the property before weekend worship or visiting.[12]

Esoteric Etiological Accounts

The etiological accounts that people tell regarding their own people and history may be called *esoteric*, since they come from within rather than from outside of the community. The type may be easiest identified in funny stories that are not meant to be taken as historical truth.

Jokes

Katie Funk Wiebe has published three joking origin stories from Russian Mennonite culture. Although preserved in America, they probably were used in Russia as well.

Q. *Where does the family name "Warkentin" come from?*

A. A stranger showed up in a Russian Mennonite village. The villagers, sitting as usual on the benches in the front of their houses at the close of the day, turned to one another and asked, "War kennt ihn (Who knows him)?" So, after the man decided to stay, he was known as Mr. Warkentin.[13]

Most likely, "Warkentin" comes from the place-name "Perkentin," in Mecklenburg. The *w/v* letter/sound in Warkentin, which substitutes for the *p* letter/sound in Perkentin, represents a regular characteristic of German dialects. This understanding of origins suggests that the Warkentins may have been Mennonites already in Prussia—before the Mennonite villages were established in Russia.[14] The origin story becomes a kind of slur against the family, since it suggests that Warkentins were strange newcomers, rather than longstanding members of the close-knit Mennonite group.

Q. *Why did the Molotschnaer speak a Low German dialect that differed from that of the Chortitzer?*

A. These two colonies spoke variations of the same Low German dialect, the Chortitzer using more inflectional endings than the Molotschnaer. Tradition has it that when God was giving instructions to the people of the earth at the time of creation, the Old Colonists crowded close to him to get precise instructions about their future. Those who carelessly stood far away did not hear the word-endings and have never spoken as pure a language.[15]

Q. *Why did the Chortitzer make grote Tweback, or big buns?*

A. The settlers in the two mother colonies in Southern Russia, Molotschna and Chortitza, visited with one another whenever possible, sharing one another's hospitality. Chortitza was known for its excellent buns, so before visitors from Molotschna returned home they stuffed their pockets with them. The Chortitzer soon caught on and learned to bake their buns so large they wouldn't fit into pockets, starting the tradition of the grote Tweback, or big buns.[16]

These are rich origin stories. The first one, for instance, has a whimsical sense of being at the original Creation, which connects it in a parodic manner with the Hebrew Genesis accounts and the more humble Anansi creation stories from Africa. Culturally, both stories are also concerned with the origin of the Russian Mennonite colonies ("two mother colonies") and, in fact, betray a traditional rivalry that probably existed from the original move from Prussia to Ukraine. Recently Jack Thiessen has persuasively demonstrated that the differences in the Molotchna and Chortitza dialects come from dialect differences still observable in the Vistula Delta homelands of both groups of Mennonite colonists.[17] The different sizes of the Moltschna and Chortitza buns may have similar cultural origins.

In folkloric terms these two stories are ethnic slurs (chapter 2), apparently told by Chortitzer at the expense of their neighbors and cultural rivals, the Molotschnaer. The first story proves that the Molotschnaer were farther from God, less cultured, and less forward-looking; the second proves that they were greedy spongers. In both cases the Chortitzer are depicted as smarter.

The stories cannot be dismissed as mere entertainment since their deeper social function was to preserve—and perhaps also create—social discriminations.

Beliefs

"Folk belief," a term that includes superstitions, refers to understandings about nature and human nature that are not based on scientific demonstration but, rather, on traditional beliefs and attitudes inherited from a community that has accepted and endorsed them over time.

Q. *Why do the Indiana Amish often have pet peacocks in their farmyards?*

A. Because the peacocks make so much noise that they scare away trespassers.[18]

This Amish answer is indeed plausible, although it is doubtful that peacocks can serve such a protective function better than dogs. More likely, Amish raise peacocks because it has been a custom among many farmers to mix in exotic items just for fun. Good examples would be guinea fowl and multicolored Indian corn, both of which are more decorative than useful. The Amish answer gives a practical justification for a custom that otherwise is related to luxury. The Amish who raise peacocks may do so because they like exotic, colorful things to brighten the drab colors required in other areas of their lives.

Five etiological beliefs connect contemporary Mennonite, Hutterite, and Amish experience with early years of persecution.

Q. *When the Amish of northern Indiana stand for the reading of the Scriptures during worship services, why do the women face the wall instead of the reader?*

A. Because during the early years of persecution some members of the congregation always had to be looking out of the windows to see whether any of their enemies were coming.

Q. *In early Dutch Mennonite churches, why did the women sit in a square in the middle and the men in benches surrounding the square?*

A. So the men could warn and protect the women in case authorities came to arrest them.[19]

Q. *Why do Hutterites sing so loudly?*

A. Because their persecuted ancestors used to sing loudly in jail so that they could be heard from cell to cell.[20]

Q. *Why do the Amish sing their hymns so slowly?*

A. Because when the persecuted Anabaptists were in prison, they sang slow tunes so that other people in the prison would not dance while they sang.[21]

Q. *Why does the* Ausbund *have red sprinkles on the fore edges, and why does the* Unparteiisch Liedersammlung *have red on the fore edges?*

A. The red colorings "represent the blood that was shed thru the [persecutions] and the songs and hymns in these two books were most all written by the [persecuted Anabaptists]."[22]

All five explanations, of course, show how deeply ingrained in Anabaptist groups is the remembrance—even though vague—of the early years of persecution, as recorded in *Martyrs Mirror*.

Such traditional, persistent beliefs are powerful testimony to the martyr complex that modern Anabaptists are said to bear. Although the queries may have no "correct" answers, there are plausible alternative explanations for each one.

One very practical reason why Indiana Amish women face the wall during scripture-reading may be related to the seating arrangement in Indiana Amish worship services. When meeting in some Amish homes, men sit in one block, women in another, with the two groups facing each other. If the women did not turn away when standing, the women and men in the front rows would be uncommonly, embarrassingly close to each other.[23] However, knowledge of customs in the worship services of other Amish communities suggests something different. In Amish worship services in Lancaster County, both men and women face away from the preacher during the reading of scripture. Holmes County, Ohio, practice resembles that found in northern Indiana, with men facing the reader and women facing away from him. However, in the Milverton, Ontario, and Allen, Adams, and Daviess County, Indiana, communities, both men and women are seated during scripture reading.[24] The differing practices in the U.S. may be continuations of differing practices in Europe, depending upon when the different groups immigrated. Perhaps the standing posture reflects respect for the Scriptures, as is also found in some high-church services when worshipers stand to hear the Gospel reading. It may be tempting to think that, in northern Indiana, Amish women face the wall to show submission—both to the Scriptures and to the menfolk—although the varieties of Amish practice would not support that conclusion. The reason for facing or not facing the scripture reader cannot be known, but it is certainly unlikely that its origin lay in women facing the wall in order to detect persecutors.

Early Dutch Mennonites may have sat with men surrounding the women because the Dutch Reformed, before them, also sat like that. The practice may have been introduced among the Mennonites following an influx of Reformed converts to

Mennonites around 1618. The Dutch Reformed may indeed have adopted that arrangement to protect themselves against harassment by government authorities who interrupted their worship services in the early years.[25] Would defenseless Mennonites have arranged themselves in that same way for that same reason?

Robert Friedmann located two written accounts of Hutterite martyrs, from 1536 and 1558, who deliberately sang loudly while they were imprisoned—one of them, in fact, for the reason given above.[26] It is unknown whether Hutterites preserved this explanation throughout their history or have given it only since Friedmann's writing on the subject, but since the one account appears in the Hutterite *Chronicle*, the former may be true. It is also true that folk singing style, in general, often has a penetrating, nasal quality.

George Pullen Jackson has given plausible explanations for slow Amish singing. First, although there actually are few "long" notes in Amish singing, it seems slow because a single syllable may be given a long embellishment (melisma) of from three to nine different tones. The result is that a single stanza takes many minutes to sing. The melismas may have developed, however, from inherently slow singing. Pullen observes that "groups sing more slowly than a solo singer. And when the group is uncontrolled (by instrument, director, or notation) it drags still more." A singer who holds a note and waits for other singers to change tones will waver in his pitch. "The relief of the one tends to become the relief of the many. The many tend to waver along similar lines," thus creating melismas.[27]

The red coloring on the two Amish songbooks was originally decorative in function, being a cheaper version of gold and marbled edging. The first *Ausbund* to have red fore edges was the 1880 Lancaster edition. Since then, the coloring has been irregular, although the 1952 edition was in solid red. Prior to 1880, copies of the *Ausbund* sometimes had green marbling or gold or silver coloring. The shorter *Liedersammlung* has had red edges since 1911; the enlarged version, only once, in 1916.

Clearly, the symbolic explanation developed after the fact of the red coloring and is now used to justify the red decoration of new editions.[28]

Legends

In the study of folklore, a legend is any traditional narrative that is received as true by its audience. Although popular understanding of the term assumes that such a story is historically untrue, the folklore term refers to traditional stories that are believed to be true, whether they can or cannot be historically verified. Of course, belief is a relative thing. Some of the etiological jokes discussed above—particularly the Warkentin joke—may indeed be believed by some tellers or hearers.

Similarly, it is often difficult to separate an etiological belief from an etiological legend. The latter refers to a traditional narrative, the former, to a concept. For instance, the worship beliefs discussed above do have a vaguely narrative kernel—persecution—at their heart, although the narrative is extremely generalized.

In any event, each etiological account that follows uses more or less of a story to explain how something otherwise odd came about.

Q. *Why do the Amish use hooks and eyes instead of buttons?*

A. Well, now, the story that I got from [John Yoder] is simply that . . . the Amish did go up the Rhine [expelled from Switzerland, heading for America] and they got to Rotterdam and the boat was delayed and they were held up there by the authorities and they were misused—that is, mistreated—at times. And at least mildly prosecuted. I don't think anybody was actually killed during that stay. But they were not welcome there. . . . One of the ways they were trying to be somewhat mean to them was to cut off the buttons of their coats—so they couldn't button their coats. And in the cold weather that was very uncomfortable. And . . . these resourceful Amish went out and found wire and fashioned themselves hooks and eyes—

homemade, very crude, wire fasteners—and they stuck them through their clothes in one side and out another and they hooked them together.[29]

Here, of course, is yet another use of the tradition of persecution to explain and justify a peculiar modern practice. Two features of the story are especially revealing. First, the Amish preacher who originally told this story and occasionally uses it in sermons, gives the Amish credit for inventing hooks and eyes. Second, he also assumes that prior to this invention the Amish indeed used buttons. They abandoned them not in order to be nonconformed to the world but out of necessity; and now the nonuse of buttons is a kind of symbolic commemoration of early years of persecution.

In his authoritative study of Mennonite costume Melvin Gingerich is unable to document exactly why, historically, the Amish have preferred hooks and eyes to buttons. He does say, however, that the Amish were already using hooks and eyes at the time of the Mennonite-Amish division, and that buttons were not an issue at that time. He also implies that the Amish may have opposed buttons because of their decorative potential.[30]

The origin of names—as in the Warkentin story above—is a frequent topic of etiological legends. The following stories deal with given names, place-names, and food names.

Q. *Why are there so many boys with the English name of "Perry" in the Eli V. Yoder family?*

A. Eli V. Yoders had much wood to cut when they lived in LaGrange County, Indiana, and therefore hired English woodcutters and [Mrs. Lydia Knepp] has in her possession a bench made by her father for the woodcutters to sit on at the table, and all of the children at one time or other would sit on that bench to eat at Father's table. They had an English woodcutter named Perry, and he was so well thought of by the family that they named their first son Perry. This was the first Amish child in Indiana to bear that name. There now are a number of that name in this genealogy.[31]

Like many origin stories in family folklore, this one is preserved in a family genealogy book—a rich treasure trove for folklore collectors. Also, in family folklore it is not unusual to preserve an item of material culture (in this case, a bench) that presumably commemorates the beginning of a nonmaterial family tradition.

The legend tries to rationalize the presence of a non-German, nonbiblical name in an Amish family. But even if one assents to it as an accurate account of one family's tradition, it is harder to believe the legend's implicit claim that the English woodcutter Perry was the origin of all Amish uses of "Perry" in the naming of northern Indiana Amish boys. After all, there may have been other English Perrys who lived or associated with other Amish families.

In addition to origin stories for personal names, an even more common type attempts to explain the origin of peculiar geographical place names.

Q. *How did the crossroads settlement of Honeyville, Indiana, get its name?*

A. Well, the way Dad and Grandpa Cristner told it, there was this fellow named Will who had a store next to Bert Miller's shop in Schrock. That's what it was called then. This Will wanted bees so he'd have honey to use and to sell in his store. Of course, in those days honey was valuable. That way folks didn't have to use so much from the sugar barrel if they had honey stored away. This Will knew of a fellow farther west, toward Goshen, who had some bee trees. One night it was snowing, and I guess Will thought it was his chance to get some of those bees on the sly. So he took his team and bobsled, drove to the place where the bees were, and cut down one of the trees. Then he sawed out the chunk with the bees and headed for home. But, you see, it quit snowing about that time. And the next morning the owner saw those tracks leading out of his grove and saw what had happened. Well, he tracked Will all the way home and found the part with the bees in it back of Will's store. I don't know what he did about the stolen bees. But from then on the people around there began calling this Will "Der Honig Vill" or "Honey Will." And that's how Honeyville came to be called that, even if it's still listed on the maps as Schrock.[32]

This place-name legend was passed down by three generations of an Amish family who were early settlers in Honeyville, Indiana, a very small, predominantly Amish neighborhood in LaGrange County. Officially named "Schrock," it is almost never referred to as such by natives.

It is reasonable that German-speaking residents of a town officially named after a German family name, Schrock, would try to explain how the town nevertheless eventually took on an unofficial, English-sounding name. Even though the story rationalizes the English name, it does so by claiming that the English name "Honeyville" is actually derived from the German *Honig Will*. Hence both names preserve—and thereby vindicate—the German culture of the people in the neighborhood.

This etiological tale incorporates element of the dialect story genre and also the linguistic process of folk etymology (whereby an otherwise strange-sounding word is reinterpreted to fit the hearer's own speech patterns). In Will's nickname, "Honey," the story also reflects Amish nicknaming practices.

Q. *Why do some Amish quilts have red patches in them?*

A. Midwestern Amish women often bought fabrics from peddlers who went from home to home with their wares. A good peddler learned to know his territory and how to market his merchandise. He knew what kinds of fabrics appealed to his Amish clients and made bundles of those fabrics, offering them at a bargain rate. But among the desirables he might place some items that were slow movers. One Amish woman wanted a bundle of fabrics that contained a piece of bright red cloth. Knowing that this particular color was out of her domain, she explained to the peddler that she would like the bundle but with an exchange for the red. Apparently having had trouble moving the red elsewhere, he refused to swap. So she purchased, along with her needs, a piece that she could use only in a secondary function. This bright red cloth became quilt fabric.[33]

Notice that this account traces all Amish uses of red to "one Amish woman," which illustrates the universal desire to make origins as specific as possible.

In this explanatory legend the red in quilts becomes a token of Amish frugality—not wanting to waste a scrap—rather than a sign of their love of bright colors. Two women quoted in Judy Schroeder Tomlonson's book, *Mennonite Quilts and Pieces,* all cite practical rather than aesthetic reasons for the Amish quilters' use of red. One says that it was "very colorfast" and the other that it "didn't fade so easily."[34]

Two other women in the Tomlonson book claim connections between Amish clothing and red quilt materials. One cites a "cranberry red" Amish woman's bonnet worn around 1918,[35] implying that the red quilt scraps actually might have come from material used to make Amish clothing. Another says: "The Amish women always wore long black dresses and usually their slips weren't that long, so they had very deep hems, as much as ten inches deep. This red material was then used to form the hems, rather than use the 'good' dress material, all for modesty's sake."[36] Her explanation seems to imply that Amish women may have bought red material for quilts and then used the remainder to lengthen their slips.

This explanation suggests the plausible notion that Amish quilters used red patches simply because they liked the color. Since many Amish quilts were made from colored cloth bought specifically for quilting, one need not make a correspondence between all Amish quilt patches and Amish rules regarding colors for clothing. Indeed, red is a culturally ingrained color in Amish taste, appearing most noticeably in the typical painting schemes for older Amish furniture—as in Somerset County, Pennsylvania, usually red, black and gold.

In fact, John Joseph Stoudt quotes Dr. Schoepf, a traveler among Pennsylvania Germans in 1783, on the universal love of red that he saw in their household decorations: "A great four-cornered stove, a table in the corner with benches fastened to the wall, everything daubed with red. . . ."[37] This Germanic appreciation for red lasted longer among the ultraconservative Amish than among other German groups, and it should therefore not surprise us to find red persisting in Amish household décor, in this case quilts.

The peddler who sold the red remnants is sometimes said to have been a Jew from Fort Wayne, Indiana.[38] That dimension of the tale connects it with a family tradition reported by a student at Goshen College. Although most members of his family are light-haired and blue-eyed, occasionally a dark-complexioned Yoder appears. Family members say that is because farther back in the Swigart family tree, there was a Jewish ancestor.[39]

These two accounts, as well as the family origin story for the name "Perry," suggest that ethnically homogeneous Mennonites sometimes explain anomalous cultural features by attributing them to intrusive ethnic outsiders who alter the otherwise "pure" Amish culture. On the other hand, the student says that the family belief is often stated with pride, as if family members mean to say, "We may be Mennonites, but we are Mennonites of a special kind." This example illustrates that the true meaning of all of the items cited here always depends on the social context in which the beliefs and stories are communicated.

Chapters 1 and 4 discuss the story of Menno Simons falling into a barrel of molasses, which is an etiological legend that explains the Dutch Mennonites' proverbial sweet tooth. That story—and perhaps also the one of Menno in the stagecoach, in chapter 4, which accounts for the origin of the "Mennonite lie"—suggests that a cycle of origin stories using Menno as a creative culture-hero once circulated in Dutch Mennonite-related folk groups. If so, then the originator of the tribe, Menno, was sensed by them to have been a kind of creator deity—much as Anansi originally was by West Africans and Coyote by Native Americans. More research is needed to clarify the range and development of this tradition.

Academic Etiological Accounts

All of the etiological accounts given thus far come from oral traditions. As historical data they are suspect, because they cannot be verified through written records.

The accounts in this section show the etiological impulse at work among academic historians. The main differences from the preceding accounts are that the conclusions are the result of individual judgments, are based on documented evidence, usually in writing, and have academic reliability. In some important ways, however. they bear striking resemblances to their folk counterparts.

Q. *What is the origin of the Amish office of full deacon?*

A. No one has been able to ferret out the origins of the office of full deacon. It has no counterpart in the Mennonite Church nor in any other Anabaptist group. Old Order Amish historians and others theorize, quite plausibly, that the office was created when the Amish church in Europe was suffering persecution, so that the work of the church could go on even if the elder or full minister were imprisoned.[40]

The plausibility of the explanation is qualified by two considerations. One is that, in eighteenth-century Switzerland, the Amish, like the Mennonites, were "harassed" rather than truly "persecuted," and held in monasteries for instruction rather than "imprisoned." More interesting, of course, is that the scholarly conclusion reaches for an explanation based on persecution, as do six of the folk explanations discussed above. Since some of the authorities cited by the historian are Old Order Amish people, the explanation may derive from the same oral tradition that formed the persecution etiologies discussed earlier. Here an academically trained historian also sanctions the explanation.

Q. *Where does the diamond-in-the-square design in Pennsylvania Amish quilts come from?*

A. The design of brass embossings on old copies of the *Ausbund*.[41]

Q. *Where does the tulip design in Pennsylvania German folk art come from?*

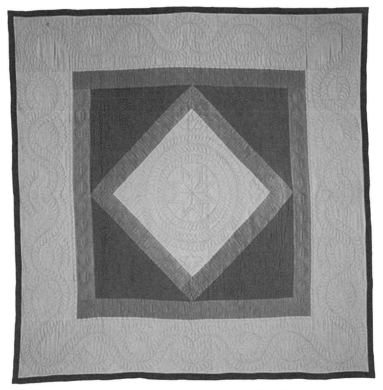

An antique Amish quilt pattern called diamond-in-the-square.

A. From a chest made for the (Mennonite) Spycher family of Oberalm near Bern, Switzerland, in 1689.[42]

In actuality, both authors cited here are more tentative about their conclusions than the statements above suggest. But both clearly prefer their understandings about origins to alternative possibilities.

These explanations tackle the almost impossible task of identifying the origins of folk art designs. The tulip, for instance, is by far too ubiquitous a flower in European and Middle Eastern culture for anyone to assume that its popular use has only one origin. Although a very early Mennonite chest with the design may have survived, the conclusion does not take into account the hundreds of other decorated chests—from all over—that may have used the tulip design earlier but have not survived.

Both explanations also attempt to find indigenous—i.e., Mennonite or Amish—sources for designs used by those people. They do not adequately acknowledge the role of borrowing in the transmission of designs from one folk group to another, or from fine art to folk art, for example. The quilt scholars acknowledge that diamond-in-the-square designs are also found in other textiles that Amish quilters may have been exposed to—namely, English quilts and Persian rugs. This tendency to seek indigenous origins for Mennonite and Amish designs may be based on the notion that Mennonites and Amish have always been separated culturally from their neighbors, whereas, in point of fact, almost no Mennonite or Amish material folk traditions are exclusive to those people. All are probably borrowed—albeit adapted to new circumstances of time, place and use (and therefore meaning).

Q. *Where does the common Mennonite and Amish family name of "Yoder" come from?*

A. The name Joder derives from the saint's name Theodore. St. Theodore was one of the missionary saints who in the early Middle Ages came up into the Swiss Alps (from Italy), bringing the message of Christ. The medieval Swiss loved their St. Theodore and in their prayers to him abbreviated his name to St. Joder.[43]

Here, again, is an origin story for a family name. In this case the scholarly research was done primarily by a distinguished American folklorist, Don Yoder, of the University of Pennsylvania. His discovery displaces the earlier family folk belief that "the Yoder name was given to our forefathers because of their talent in singing and yodeling in the Swiss Alps"[44]—a belief probably arrived at through the similarities between the two words "yodel" and "Yoder."

The research supports three additional origin beliefs. First, St. Theodore was the first bishop of Octodorus (Martigny,

Valais). Second, he brought the bell to the Valais from Italy. And, finally, his Yoder followers "were among the very early people to turn Protestant."[45]

Exactly how the name of the saint was transferred to a group of people is, of course, unknown. Most likely the Yoders simply took as their own the name of the place where they lived, whether that was the St. Joderhorn mountain or the St. Joder chapel and the village that may once have surrounded it.[46] The extended family prefers to think that the naming came from devotion to the saint, "who was held in such great esteem and affection by his people that they took his name."[47]

Whether true or false, the etymology supports certain self-perceptions among the Yoder clan. First, their origin is with a saint—not with royalty, as is the goal of so many other genealogical searchers. Second, they chose his name from pious devotion. Third, although Theodore may have been Roman Catholic, the Yoders were among the earliest Swiss Protestants. All of these implications obviously contribute to the self-concept of a historically-minded, pious Protestant clan.

Q. *What is the origin of the Swiss Brethren?*

A. The Swiss Brethren began on the evening of January 21 ("probably"), 1525, in Zurich, Switzerland, when Conrad Grebel conducted the first ceremony of adult baptism. "This was the birthday of Anabaptism."[48]

Q. *What is the origin of the Hutterites?*

A. In 1528 a group of Swiss Brethren were in flight, in persecution. And it occurred to them, if every man is for himself, we'll all perish. If we would just pool our resources and help one another to the utmost, maybe we could make it. So somebody put a blanket down and everybody put his wealth—in jewelry or money or anything—on that blanket. And sure enough they did make it.[49]

Both of these charismatic moments in Anabaptist history have become well-established facts about origins in Mennonite historiography. It is important to notice, however, that the facts are really judgments based on extremely complex data. To say that Anabaptism or the Hutterites "began" at those specific moments is, ultimately, somewhat arbitrary, since historical milestones like these are extremely complex processes, rather than isolatable moments in time.

I do not mean to imply that the judgments—and the scholarly traditions that ensue from them—are in error. I simply want to point out that both the folk and the academic conclusions spring from the same human impulse to give single-minded, clear-cut reasons and explanations for intriguing but baffling materials.

Conclusion

The foregoing can be mistakenly read as a cynical attempt to debunk some traditional notions that have been uncritically held by many people in Mennonite communities. That is true only to the extent that the discussion rightly implies that it is virtually impossible to know for sure the exact origins of many common words and customs that are lost in the mists of time. Instead of saying, "We do it because we have always done it thus," or "We do it because we like to do it this way," or "We believe this because we like to think of it like this," communities foster traditional tales and beliefs to account somehow for things that are otherwise baffling.

The alternative explanations given for the origins and causes discussed above are not necessarily more accurate or satisfying than the traditional ones. However, as equally plausible alternatives, they put into sharper focus the socially important meanings that the traditional explanations contain for members of the communities that sustain them. In other words, in light of the evidence available, which explanations have communities chosen to endorse? What view of their history is most appealing to them? How have they created or shaped the historical truth so that it has meaning for the lives they lead today? With a few exceptions, the general answer to that question seems to be this: In a way that will enhance the identity and cohesiveness of their community.

The interpretations, or meanings, given above are, of course, general and suggestive, not definitive. In Elliott Oring's terms, they are "propositional" rather than "performance" meanings.[50] That is, they are meanings suggested by the stories and beliefs in their cultural context only. They are not meanings related to actual use of the items in social contexts, whether informal conversation or platform speech—both of which would be "performance" situations.

For instance, the Russian Mennonite ethnic slurs given earlier in this chapter meant one thing when told by Molotchnaer about Chortitzers, and quite another thing when told by Chortitzer about themselves. In fact, every time they were told they meant something slightly different, depending on exactly who was telling them, where, when, why, and to whom. Like all folklore, their main value was that they created social order and social value.

Their broadest meaning may be best understood in terms of the functional anthropological views brought to folklore study by William Bascom (borrowing from Malinowski), as mentioned in chapter 1. Mennonite etiological tales and beliefs serve to validate Mennonite culture "in justifying its rituals and institutions to those who perform and observe them." Just as Malinowski observed about the function of myth in primitive culture, so the Mennonite origin tales and beliefs also "strengthen tradition and endow it with a greater value and prestige by tracing it back to a higher, better, more supernatural reality of initial events." Such folklore seems to appear "when dissatisfaction with or skepticism of an accepted pattern is expressed or doubts about it arise."[51]

Viewed thus, the Mennonite origin accounts are created or invoked to justify culturally marginal things that are under attack or suspicion for being irrelevant, embarrassing or illogical—whether that be big buns, peacocks, loud singing, hooks and eyes, red quilt patches, or the family name of Yoder. The origin accounts say, "Hey! That's all right after all, now that we have a historical explanation for it."

Such traditional history may not satisfy the academic historian, except as a kind of quaint curiosity. But in some ways it is a more important kind of history because it is known and shared broadly within a community and controls the way people feel, think, and act.

·4·

Trickster Tales

American Mennonites nurture an apparently unique tradition of trickster narratives. Traceable to the origins of Mennonites in Western Europe 480 years ago, the tradition may derive from their historic refusal to swear oaths and their related emphasis on truth-telling in everyday affairs. Apparently their trickster stories reflect and vindicate the strategies that Mennonites resort to in order to survive in a world where absolute truth-telling remains impractical and, at times, even life-threatening.

Many persistent features of the Mennonite experience create the right context for a trickster tradition to flourish. Chief among them is the socially marginal role that Mennonites have played in almost every country in which they have lived.[1] Modern Mennonites, of course, are direct descendants of the Anabaptist movement—the "left wing" of the Reformation—which originated in Switzerland in 1525 but subsequently sprang up in many other places in Western Europe before consolidating into the three main surviving streams: the Swiss Brethren in Switzerland, the followers of Menno Simons in the Lowlands, and the Hutterites in Moravia.

This Anabaptism became a proscribed, underground movement almost immediately after its beginning. The Anabaptists' radical positions on adult baptism, nonresistance, foreswearing of oaths, and separation of church and state put them in blatant conflict with the established order. For these heresies they were brutally persecuted by Lutherans, Calvinists and, especially,

Roman Catholics. Between their origins in 1525 and the last martyrdom in 1614, over 4,000 Anabaptist were burned at the stake, drowned, or otherwise tortured to death.[2] A once-burgeoning movement of boldly prophetic people was reduced through persecution to a shrunken band of quiet believers in an underground church. Out of this early European experience arose the martyrs' stories, the first important tradition of Mennonite oral narrative. Many of these Low Church saints' lives were eventually compiled in *The Bloody Theater or Martyrs Mirror*,[3] a huge tome still kept next to the Bible in many Mennonite homes.

In America the Mennonite experience has been somewhat different.[4] Less prophetic and evangelistic in their program, American Mennonites have tended to be "die Stillen im Lande" (the quiet in the land), cultivating the land and in-group virtues. According to one Mennonite historian, their greatest achievement in America has been survival.[5] Despite their prosperity, Mennonites have been on the fringes of mainstream American culture. Earlier that was because they spoke German, opposed slavery, were conscientious objectors throughout all of America's wars and, through clothing and other customs, assumed a nonconformist stance toward popular culture. Today they remain a marginal people because of their critique of nationalism, particularly militarism, nuclear weaponry, and draft registration.

Because they have barely survived within a hostile culture, Mennonites might logically be expected to nurture a tradition of trickster tales in their oral lore. After all, the underdog mentality almost universally produces a diminished but clever hero who, through trickery, barely makes his way through life.

On the other hand, even the slightest acquaintance with Anabaptist history and theology undermines that assumption, given the Mennonite emphasis on integrity of speech as embodied in their historic refusal to swear oaths. Anabaptist martyrs died in defense of this position. Menno Simons (c. 1496-1561), who spoke boldly on behalf of the principle, linked it closely with martyrdom:

In case a man's yea and nay is not kept, let him be punished as a perjurer. That yea is Amen with all true Christians is sufficiently shown by those who in our Netherlands are so tyrannically visited with imprisonment, confiscation, and torture; with fire, the stake, and the sword; while with one word they could escape all these if they would but break their yea and nay. But since they are born of the truth, therefore they walk in the truth, and testify to the truth unto death, as may be abundantly seen in Flanders, Brabant, Holland, West Friesland, etc.[6]

The nonswearing of the oath is endorsed by every Mennonite confession of faith,[7] and is, in addition to adult baptism, the only other doctrine that still unites all churches that bear the name "Mennonite."[8] Of all people—with the exception perhaps of Quakers and Brethren—one would not expect Mennonites to develop a cycle of tales that glorify the deceiver. In this case, however, social realism—or the archetypal urge—wins out over official theology and creates a trickster hero of a distinct character, inhibited as he apparently is by Mennonites' official position on honest speech.

The American Mennonite Trickster Tradition

The general outlines of that narrative tradition are suggested by three trickster tales (all told in 1983) connected with different periods of American history—the early nineteenth century, the Civil War, and the 1940s:

I don't know if this story is true or not, but they say that Peter Krehbiel was on a—probably—Conestoga wagon going toward Philadelphia with wheat. His grandson was sitting there with him. . . . It was in the winter and the ruts were frozen. And once you . . . were in the ruts you were committed for a while. But here came a fellow coming the other way. Probably not a Mennonite. Somebody had to give, and so I'm afraid Peter Krehbiel joined this conversation that went something like this: "Get out of the way!" The other one said, "No, you get out of the way!" "Back up!" "No, you back up!" And then, we're told that Peter Krehbiel said, "Listen! If you don't back up, I'm going to do something I don't want to do!" Well, the non-Mennonite backed up. And down toward Philadelphia they went. And then of course this made the next generation curious. So the grandson, he said, "Grandpa," he said, "what would you have done if that man wouldn't have done that?" He said, "Well, I'd have backed up."[9]

[Henry Brunk] was a young married man. He was a fugitive from the draft in Virginia—Shenandoah Valley—and was hiding in attics in houses, making baskets, and came out occasionally at night. And one time a man who had set out to find him met him on the road and asked whether he knew Henry Brunk. And the man should have recognized him because he was an acquaintance, but he didn't recognize him. . . . I don't know how the man phrased the question, but Henry Brunk replied, "Well, why don't you go down to this neighbor down here. He probably knows something about it." . . . Just diverted the fellow and the fellow went down. And Henry Brunk got away after that—fled out of the valley.

When . . . westerners had to get out of China, J. Lawrence Burkholder [relief worker and amateur pilot] was late—one of the last ones at the airport to get out. . . . But they said, "Wait, you can't go out." And he says, "Well, I'm a pilot." And he pointed to the plane out there and—and he got out.

Two features of these stories are crucial to the Mennonite trickster tradition. Both are related to truth-telling.

First, all are legends. They are personal legends—anecdotes told as true about well-known people in the Mennonite community. In chapter 5 I make a case for a pronounced preference for legend as opposed to tales among Mennonites, specifically because of their historically ingrained emphasis on telling the truth. Only a handful of trickster stories in my collection are traditional folk tales applied to "a Mennonite." The rest are personal legends.

Second, the Mennonite tricksters technically do not lie. Their replies are literally truthful, yet evasive enough to achieve the desired end. The superficial subject of each story is indeed culturally "Mennonite"—farm economy, nonresistance, foreign relief work—but the deeper Mennonite substance is the avoidance of the lie. Only one story in my collection depicts a Mennonite trickster in an outright lie. In all of the rest he wins out through ambiguous silence, gesture, or verbal statement.

Of course, even the classic trickster does not always, or even most of the time, blatantly lie to achieve his end. Brer Rabbit's "Don't throw me into the brier patch!" is no lie. Only Brer Fox's thinking makes it so. But the avoidance of an outright lie—of telling the truth while not telling the truth—is simply a more crucial issue for the Mennonite teller and his audience than it is for people of other ethnic groups. And because more is at stake morally, the discrepancy between ideal and reality increases the humor in the strategy of such tales for Mennonites.

There is even a distinctive trickster cycle in Mennonite folklore. It involves a special hero—the Mennonite man wearing the "plain" or "straight-cut" coat, which somewhat resembles the coat of a Catholic priest.[10] Now virtually abandoned, except by a few conservative Mennonite groups, the plain coat was regulation apparel in some Mennonite conferences for all men in dress-up situations, in other conferences for all ministers in dress-up situations. Only in the recent years of its decline has it been regarded as other Protestant groups regard the clergyman's collar, that is, as regulation apparel when the minister is in the pulpit or carrying out other official duties.

One story about a layman outlines the cycle:

> Earl [Lehman] was in Chicago and he went by a Catholic church one evening. And he saw there was an enormous crowd in the basement. So he went in. They were having a

bingo party. And there was a policeman standing there. So . . .
Earl Lehman kind of sidled up to the policeman and he said,
"Is this legal?" And the policeman said, "Not really, Father.[11]
But . . ." he said, "if you want to start a bingo in your church,
just let me know. I know the ropes."

Three features of the plain-coated trickster cycle emerge in
that story.

First, the plain-coated Mennonite—a layman in this case—
is mistaken for a Roman Catholic priest. Never is he mistaken
for a clergyman of another Protestant denomination. It is
always Mennonite versus Catholic.

Second, the plain-coated trickster is a very passive hero—
even more so than the heroes of the first three stories. Like the
classic picaresque trickster, he may be "moving along"[12] but
he is not even expecting trouble, let alone ready to stir it up.
He does not plan to be deceptive. In fact, in this case he actually does nothing deceptive at all. The coat speaks—falsely—
for itself.

Finally, this trickster accepts, without protest, personal benefit from the silent deception. In this story he receives the useful
information of how Catholics use the legal system for their own
advantage—perhaps in order to begin his own Mennonite bingo
operation!

Within this cycle of the plain-coated Mennonite mistaken
for a Catholic is an even more specialized cycle, this time fea-
turing a plain-coated Mennonite minister who is speeding down
the highway or in some other way breaking, or potentially
breaking, the law of the land.

It is a story that M. C. Lehman used to tell—that he was
driving in Elkhart and he got stopped for going through a red
light or something. And the cop, when he saw he was a
Catholic, left him off. But he said, "Be careful at the next
intersection, because that man is not a Catholic." Now
whether that's true or not, M. C. told it.

The force of this paradigm is so powerful among Mennonites that it has generated this story:

> [John Mosemann Jr.] told Dad, I guess, that one time he was caught for speeding between Gary and South Bend. And the policeman took . . . one look at his plain coat and he said, "Oh, that's all right, Father. We know you don't want to be late for the game." And let him go. He was assuming that he was headed for the Notre Dame game, because it was scheduled for that afternoon.

Ordinary enough in terms of the cycle of which it is a part, the story is extraordinary in terms of the actual event from which it derives. John Mosemann, long-time pastor of (Goshen) College Mennonite Church, said what really happened:

> I was taking a group of [Goshen Biblical] Seminary students to Chicago for a workshop. We were traveling—is it [U.S. Route] 20? (this is a long time ago)—that skirts the northern edge of Gary and for some miles seems to be out in the country and not actually in the city limits. And suddenly I was waved off by a motorcycle officer . . . who swaggered back to our car and told me how fast I was going, which I couldn't have verified at all. I had passed so . . . many vehicles since the last . . . traffic light. And, "You are under arrest. And you'll need to follow me into Gary." I told him that I had no awareness of actually passing other cars or exceeding the speed limit. We were visiting. As far as I was aware, we were following in the line of traffic. "Well, you were exceeding the limit and so you will have to follow me back in. Have you ever conducted a funeral of an accident victim?" "No." "Well, that's strange." And I hadn't by that time. I have since—several of them. But, "I'm a good Catholic, too," he said. "But you fellows from Notre Dame think you're just a little better than the rest of us. You think you can look down your nose at us. Every Saturday after a football game we have to arrest a lot of people along here for

speeding, and a lot of them are priests. You're under arrest. You, you follow me back into Gary." "All right," I said, "I'll do that. However, I don't want you to be under any wrong impressions. I'm not a Catholic priest. I'm a Protestant minister." "Oh, well, then, go ahead!"

Here we see how the Mennonite folk imagination has converted a good-enough, true story into one that more accurately fits the folk notion of what a Mennonite speeding-preacher story *should* really be like.

As personal legends, these stories tend to gravitate toward the most prominent plain-coated preachers on the horizon. Until his death in 1995 that meant J. C. Wenger (b. 1910), a beloved Mennonite theologian, historian, and raconteur who always wore a plain coat. Here are three stories told about him as a trickster-on-the move:

There's one they tell in Scottdale [Pennsylvania] about J. C. Wenger driving from Indiana to Pennsylvania and going through Ohio. The Ohio Turnpike was kind of notorious for speed traps and he was driving along in his plain coat. And he got pulled over by a policeman and the policeman walked up to the window and said, "Oh, Father, I'm sorry to have stopped you." And J. C. Wenger said, "That's OK. You're forgiven," and drove on.

Another time J. C. Wenger was in South Bend. He was driving his car and he happened to go through a red light. Traffic cop came along and . . . stopped him—was there all ready to write out a ticket. Then he happened to look at J. C. and saw his straight coat and said, "Oh, excuse me! Are you a Father?" And J. C. says, "Well, yes, I have two sons and a daughter."

As the story goes, J. C. Wenger decided to go [by train] to Chicago one day, and he took his two little boys along. And at South Bend two [Catholic] sisters got on, from St.

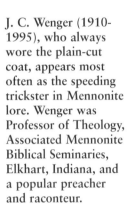

J. C. Wenger (1910-1995), who always wore the plain-cut coat, appears most often as the speeding trickster in Mennonite lore. Wenger was Professor of Theology, Associated Mennonite Biblical Seminaries, Elkhart, Indiana, and a popular preacher and raconteur.

Mary's [College]. They sat on the other side of the aisle and finally one of them looked over at J. C. and said, "How are you, Father?" He said, "Fine." And she said, "And whose little boys are these?" Only as J. C. can laugh and grin—he looked at her and said, "They're mine."

According to J. C., none of these episodes ever happened to him. However, he does tell one story in which he was the plain-coated preacher-trickster in real life:

> I was coming home from Canada with Harry Martens . . . and C. J. Dyck . . . and these two other men were sitting in the front . . . and I was sitting in the back seat. And I hap-

pened to have on the [plain-coat] garb. . . . Then we got to
the customs and the customs man was evidently a Catholic.
He spied me in the back seat. He said, "Are you smuggling
anything today, Father?" Then he put his head back and
roared. He thought his joke was so funny. And waved us on
by. So nobody had to declare anything.

Of course, the tradition is not as neatly consistent as these
examples suggest. Three final ones depict a wider range of conclusions and the interplay between fiction and reality.

As in the story by John Mosemann, occasionally an obses-
sively truthful preacher speaks up boldly instead of capitalizing
on his privileged position:

> [Jesse Short, pastor of Central Mennonite Church,
> Archbold, Ohio] was moving at a pretty good clip. Then he
> got off the turnpike and got on smaller roads to get to his
> home. And after a while he noticed in the mirror there was a
> car behind him. If he went fast, that guy went fast. And he
> thought, "I'll show you a thing or two." So he really stepped
> on it. And after a bit the guy behind him put on the siren. It
> was an unmarked police car. And the policeman came for-
> ward and asked to see his license. And it said, "Rev. Jesse J.
> Short." "Well," the policeman said, "I sure hate to arrest a
> minister. What would you do under these circumstances?"
> Jesse said, "I'd throw the book at you." And the policeman
> was so impressed he came to hear Jesse preach!

In terms of American sociology, the story testifies to the
privileged position of a clergyman of any denomination, since
Jesse Short could be identified as a minister only by his driver's
license, not by a plain coat. But, more important, it testifies to
the fact that in Mennonite storytelling the minister must win in
an encounter with the law. The storyteller glosses over whether
or not Jesse Short was arrested. Instead, he emphasizes Short's
finer, spiritual victory in attracting the policeman to a church

service. Most Mennonite trickster tales are grounded in a morality of survival; only this one hints at the grander, socially redemptive function of absolute truth-telling.

One freakish story does show the Mennonite preacher defeated by his adversary. In this story, which I have pieced together from the recollections of several people, the Mennonite preacher is stopped for speeding by a policeman, who asks him why he was going so fast. "The King's business required haste," says the preacher, quoting 1 Samuel 21:8. Often the story ends there, the preacher having saved his neck by invoking the authority of Scripture. But sometimes the policeman has the last word. He, in turn, quotes Proverbs 13:1: "But the way of trans-gressors is hard"—and arrests the minister. Even though the story is sometimes attached to a well-known, plain-coated min-ister, both its structural parallelism and its fixed punch lines associate it with the joke tradition, which helps account for its more cynical view of American Mennonite reality.

Finally, one story shows how narrative tradition leads to enactment of these trickster tales in real life:

> When [Peter Wiebe] came to Kansas as a minister he wore a plain coat. And Earl Buckwalter also wore a plain coat. And they had a [breakfast meeting] one day and [Peter Wiebe] said to Earl, "Did you ever get a free meal because you wore a plain coat and they thought you were a priest?" And Earl said, "Yes, many a time." Peter said, "I never got a one." So from that breakfast . . . meeting, Earl slipped out early and he paid Peter's breakfast. Then when Peter came to pay up, the cashier said, "There's no charge, Father." Then he was telling that story all day long, having a lot of fun. And then in the evening they had another meeting and Earl let it be known what actually happened.

It is not easy to match these Mennonite trickster tales with other, related traditions in folk narrative. Perhaps some of these Mennonite stories are denominationally specific variants of an as yet unidentified American joke cycle about the clergyman's collar in general. For instance, Mac E. Barrick[13] has collected a story that also shows a policeman excusing a driver who wears a Catholic priest's coat:

> A priest and a rabbi each received a new car as a gift from their congregations. Going through the Holland Tunnel, they met and started to race. The rabbi got ahead of the priest and had to slow down when suddenly the priest smashed into him. A big Irish cop came over and asked the rabbi for his license, then walked back to the second car. Seeing the priest's collar, he said: "How fast was this fellow going when he backed into you, Father?"

But even if this tradition is further documented, the Mennonite equivalent will probably remain unique because of the mistaken identity involved and because the Mennonite stories are personal legends closely intertwined with everyday experiences.

Studied in terms of the trickster tradition in general, the uniqueness of the Mennonite hero comes into clearer focus. As currently understood, of course, the classic trickster figure is so amorphous, so paradoxical as to render almost useless the single term— "trickster"—to cover all of his behaviors. As Roger Abrahams points out, "at various times [the trickster] is clown, fool, jokester, initiate, culture hero, even ogre."[14] Paul Radin more neatly dichotomizes the trickster's role, saying that he is "at one and the same time, creator and destroyer, giver and negator, he who dupes and who is always duped himself."[15] However, the American Mennonite trickster is not all of these. Rather, in his more specialized conduct he illustrates again how "the figure recurs in different cultures in response to different focuses and artistic conventions."[16] This is understood best through contrasting the Mennonite trickster with other American religious tricksters.

The plain-coated preacher differs considerably from the

Swedish-American preacher[17] and the Mormon heroes,
J. Golden Kimball,[18] and the missionary tricksters[19]—none of
whom is particularly deceptive.

Rather, Kimball and the Mormon missionaries are tricksters
who—primarily as clowns and smart alecks—render ridiculous
many Mormon values. The Swedish-American preacher inadvertently creates a more specialized offense through his language gaffes that introduce obscenity and blasphemy onto
sacred ground. Since we assume that these tricksters behave "as
the members of the society would behave if they were not con-
strained by fear from acting," they serve "primarily as a release
valve"[20] for the repressed desires of the Mormons and
Lutherans who tell and enjoy the stories. The special nature of
these religious tricksters probably is determined by the fact that
their identities arise primarily from their interaction with members of their own group, which may suggest that their Mormon
and Lutheran constituencies are more obsessed with esoteric
than with exoteric concerns.

On the other hand, the identities of the plain-coated
Mennonite and the Jewish-American rabbi[21] are defined
through interaction with members of outside groups, over
whom they gain the upper hand through some kind of conflict.
They resemble the deceiving heroes of underdog cultures—such
as Brer Rabbit and John among African-Americans—more so
than do Kimball, the Mormon missionary and the Swedish-
American preacher. The rabbi's success, however, is always verbal and intellectual. He has the last, smartest, best word in a
conversational interchange with an ethnic rival. His social status is thereby enhanced.

The Mennonite's success lies more in what he does than in
what he says. In one respect, of course, he does nothing at all.
He merely observes his opponent placing the wrong "frame" on
his experience, to use Irving Goffman's terminology.[22] Yet the
passive Mennonite is nevertheless a deceptive trickster insofar
as he is fully aware of the framing error being made, does not
volunteer to correct it, and receives personal benefit from the

error. In fact, he is more literally a tricky deceiver than are any of his American religious counterparts—which is impressive in light of the truth-obsessed Mennonite culture that fosters the tradition.

Of course, the classic trickster often does embody his group's strongest taboos—particularly a "release-valve" trickster like Kimball, whose appeal derives from his enactment of Mormon taboos. The Mennonite trickster's relationship to taboo is somewhat different, however. He interprets the taboo in a manner that enables him to succeed in his exoteric contacts while at the same time satisfying the moral code of his esoteric relationships.

The Dutch Mennonite Trickster Tradition

The American Mennonite trickster tales strike their deepest resonances in the context of folk narratives from a much earlier Dutch Mennonite tradition. In fact, the typical Mennonite trickster tale—the speeding preacher story—resembles in a most uncanny way an old story about Menno Simons, the most important Dutch Anabaptist leader. If American Mennonites know any story about Menno, it is this one, as told by J. C. Wenger himself:

> I think I ought to tell you one little anecdote from Menno Simons. John Horsch was a great Mennonite historian and pretty rigid in some ways and he said he can't believe it happened. But we have pretty good evidence that it did happen. Menno was riding on a stagecoach one time and instead of being in the coach he was riding up front, up high, with the driver. And the authorities dashed up on horses to arrest Menno if they could find him. And they said, "Is Menno Simons in that coach?" And Menno turned around and yelled into the coach, "Is Menno Simons in there?" And they said, "No, he's not in here." So Menno told the authorities, "They say Menno's not in the coach." So he lived to die in bed.

The story is undoubtedly traditional. Before becoming attached to Menno it was told about Hans Buscher, an Anabaptist preacher from Antwerp.[23] A similar story is told about John Bunyan in England,[24] which suggests that variants are told about many religious leaders.

The story of Menno on the coach contains features almost identical to the American stories of the plain-coated preacher: the Mennonite hero is "going along" the road; he is stopped by authorities, in both cases Catholic; his life or freedom is threatened; he gives an evasive response; and he accepts undeserved benefits without demur. The major difference, of course, is the issue at stake. In the speeding preacher story it is merely a traffic fine; in Menno's case it is his life. The juxtaposed stories do reveal an apparently universal Mennonite sense of being in opposition to the law of the land, even though that is qualified in tolerant America by a greater—but not total—Mennonite accommodation to mainstream culture.

The Dutch Mennonite context in which the Menno Simons story has thrived clarifies the cultural implications of that story as well as the stories currently found in the United States. The best data for this understanding come from an essay long neglected in Anabaptist studies: J. G. de Hoop Scheffer's "Mennisten-streken [Mennonite Tricks]," in the 1868 issue of *Doopsgezinde Bijdragen*. Scheffer uses the coach story along with seven other accounts—some from *Martyrs Mirror*—in trying to explain why members of other religious groups in Europe have regarded Dutch Mennonites as deceivers, or tricksters.

He points out that the phrase "Mennonite tricks" was used proverbially to refer to Mennonites in the same way that "pigheaded" was used to characterize Lutherans, "bigoted" was used for Calvinists, and "light troops" was used for Huguenots and Remonstrants.[25] Scheffer's work thus highlights an inherent contradiction in esoteric and exoteric perceptions of Mennonite truth-telling: in esoteric Mennonite lore Mennonites are scrupulously honest; in the exoteric lore of non-Mennonites, Mennonites are archdeceivers.

Scheffer defines "Mennonite tricks" as follows:

> To say a truth and to withhold a truth, and then especially to say half the truth and appear that the truth has been told completely; to evade the answer on a question and yet give the person who asks the impression that nothing is lacking in the answer—that is what non-Mennonites label with the term "Mennonite tricks."[26]

His definition fits perfectly the kind of truthful lie-telling observable in the ethic of the modern American Mennonite trickster.

Scheffer offers several explanations for the development of this reputation. He points out that the admonition, "Let your communication be yea, yea" (Matt. 5:37), made such an impact upon the character of Dutch Mennonites that they hesitated to say a definite "yes" or "no" to questions involving their future actions, since they could not honestly be certain that they could be faithful to their word.[27] Instead, they conveyed "yes" or "no"' by indirections, often by a certain inflection in their speech. Their Lutheran and Reformed neighbors, unacquainted with the implications of their refusal to swear oaths, wrongly interpreted Mennonites' responses as sneaky equivocation.[28]

Scheffer also claims that this reputation derives, in part, from the strategy that the earliest Anabaptists developed in order to cope with persecution. They soon resorted to having baptizers, whose names were unrevealed to the baptismal candidates, baptize adults whose names were unknown to the baptizers. Consequently, both the baptizers and the baptized could honestly say to their inquisitors, "I do not know," when asked the identity of other people involved in the proscribed ritual. In addition, when subjected to inquisition, Anabaptists spoke clearly and boldly about their religious convictions. But they were often silent, evasive, or even somewhat equivocating about the details of their associations with other people, lest they incriminate fellow believers. After all, they said, Christ himself remained silent before Pilate, and Christ also cautioned his disciples to be "careful as serpents." Scheffer adds, "Courage does not exclude cleverness."[29]

Although American Mennonites are nearly four centuries removed from their European origins, and although the Mennonites from whom I collected most of my stories are of Swiss, German, or Alsatian rather than Dutch origin, the continuity of ethnic traits and storytelling motifs from one time and place to another is impressive indeed.

Aside from using the story of Menno on the coach first in his analysis, Scheffer gives it no special attention. However, we are surely justified in regarding it as an etiological legend. That is, the story contains the original pattern of conduct that Mennonites have been imitating ever since.

The only literal evidence for such a judgment resides in the Dutch playing card game *Doopsgezind Kwartetspel* (Mennonite Quartet Game). The card representing the proverbial phrase "Menniste Leugen [Mennonite lie]" is illustrated with a drawing of Menno on the coach, which implies that that story is the prototype for the proverb and the ethnic trait.[30]

More evidence can be added from a complementary legend about Menno that is explicitly etiological (and is also cited in chapter 1):

> Menno was preaching in a barn. And as was the custom, the women sat in the center and the men around the outside to protect them, as was typical of the churches in that day as well. And . . . there was a shout outside that the sheriff had come to arrest him. So the men barred the way. And Menno was standing on a molasses barrel for his pulpit, and in his haste to get down, the end of the barrel caved in and he sank to his knees in molasses and would have laid a gooey track in escaping. And so all the women in the front row each took one long lick of molasses off his hosen [leggings]. And that explains why Mennonite children in Holland to this day have a sweet tooth.[31]

Drawings of Menno Simons in the coach and in the molasses barrel by artist T. Schaap-Stuurman. Illustrations of the "Mennonite Lie" and the "Mennonite Sweet Tooth" from the Dutch Mennonite card game printed by Firma J. Roggeband.

In the playing card game referred to above, a drawing of this story illustrates the card dedicated to the other proverbial phrase, "Menniste Zoet [Mennonite sweet]." Within such a narrative context, Menno Simons himself becomes the archetypal, original Mennonite trickster par excellence. He illustrates the wider range of trickster behavior—including creation and buffoonery—that Abrahams and Radin describe, but that the plaincoated American trickster himself lacks. In the coach story Menno is the technically innocent deceiver.

In the molasses story, and possibly also in the coach story, he is the creator, the quasi-divine figure near the creative origins of Mennonitism who established the special gifts of the tribe— the sweet truth and the ability to survive. And in his bumbling behavior in the molasses story he is the foolish buffoon as well.

His identity as deceiver arises from exoteric Mennonite lore, in other words, from a story showing Menno interacting with outsiders. His identity as creator and buffoon arises from esoteric lore, in other words, from a story showing Menno interacting with his own people. The American plain-coated preacher is his contemporary counterpart as deceiver; his contemporary equivalent as clown may be discovered through further study of American Mennonite storytelling.

Since I collected most of my stories in rather artificial settings, I have been unable to study the functions that they serve in ordinary conversational flow.[32] Considering the gap between the Mennonite ideal of truthfulness and the trickster reality of deception, one might assume that on the whole they serve primarily a compensatory function. That is, Mennonites tell such stories as a socially sanctioned way of coping with a moral obligation that at times is oppressive. However, it seems more accurate to assume that the trickster stories validate Mennonite culture—not Mennonite theology but the compromised *culture* that has emerged in applying ideal to reality. Both the etiological nature of the Menno Simons story and the fact that most of the other stories are regarded as true by their tellers support this judgment. In this light, the Mennonite trickster tales embody the strategy that has enabled Mennonites to survive, even flourish.

The truly Anabaptist calling is a difficult, punishing, almost impossible one. Mennonites are expected to take literally the "hard sayings" of Jesus, not only in belief but also in practice. The alternatives are starkly contrasted: Obedience to the literal commands may lead to death; disobedience may lead to damnation.

A plain-coat story from the American Amish experience illustrates the schizophrenic impulses that such tension produces:

> This one came up, of the Amish man who sold his tobacco to the tobacco warehouse in Lancaster. . . . And the tobacco-buyer was taking advantage of him . . . knowing that this

Amishman was likely not [to] be too belligerent and so on—
at least profession-wise he would claim not to be. But it came
to the place where [the Amish man] took off his coat, his
plain coat, and threw it down: "Dere is the Amish man. Here
is Stoltzfus. You give me my money!"[33]

Some people claim that American Mennonites still bear a
martyr complex, whether from ancient memories or from fear
of what will happen to defenseless Christians during the next
war. Like all human beings, they look for a satisfactory way out.
There are alternatives to being burned alive, as the following
story suggests:

> The morning lecture on tour was about the persecuted
> Anabaptists once again. This time [David Joris] had fled to
> Basel, Switzerland, for refuge, where he changed his name,
> and in time, became a respected and wealthy citizen. At his
> funeral, the citizens of the city eulogized the man's contribu-
> tion to the country. About five years later the city fathers
> accidentally discovered that the man they had buried with
> such glowing words was actually a hated and once much-
> sought-after Anabaptist. They dug up his remains and burned
> them publicly at the stake. Said the Mennonite tourist:
> "That's [the] way I'd like to be burned at the stake!"[34]

David Joris (c. 1501-56) was more aggressively deceptive
than the heroes of the other stories surveyed in this chapter. But
the tourist's response is what nourishes the Mennonite trickster
tradition. It may not be exactly what Menno Simons had in
mind in his writings on the oath. And it may not be what martyrs who died for refusing to swear the oath would endorse. But
it is vindicated by what Menno himself actually did (so they
say). And it even fulfills the mysterious command of the Savior
in Matthew 10:16: "Behold, I send you forth as sheep in the
midst of wolves; be ye therefore wise as serpents and harmless
as doves."

·5·

The Reggie Jackson Urban Legend

From about March through August of 1982, people in Mennnonite communities in the United States and Canada enjoyed hearing and telling as true the story of how Reggie Jackson, baseball superstar, inadvertently intimidated three Mennonite women in the elevator of a New York City hotel. Although most Mennonites were unaware of the fact, a culturally less specific version of the story had also captured the imagination of non-Mennonite America, beginning about two years earlier, with printed versions of it appearing in city newspapers from early January through September of 1982.[1] As of 2004, the story rarely surfaces in Mennonite groups, although it remains one of the most "durable and popular" stories of its type in the U.S. today, according to folklorist Jan Brunvand.[2]

The story is an urban legend: "A story in a contemporary setting (not necessarily a big city), reported as a true individual experience, with traditional variants that indicate its legendary character."[3]

Other, more familiar examples of the genre include stories about the new car that can be bought cheap because a corpse decayed in it, the alligators in the sewer system of New York City, and the cat or rat meat found in the food served at the ethnic or fast food restaurant just down the street.[4] The Reggie Jackson legend received full consideration in Brunvand's second book on urban legends *The Choking Doberman* (1984). There it is linked with the title story, which concerns a white woman who finds her dog choking on the bitten-off fingers of a black housebreaker later found hiding in an upstairs closet. Both stories share the motifs of a dog, a black intruder, and a frightened white woman.[5]

Brunvand's discussion of the Reggie Jackson story shows that Mennonites' use of it was only a footnote in the widespread American interest in the story. However, the Mennonite circulation of the story was so enthusiastic and so culturally distinctive that it prompts a detailed analysis of how a folk group appropriates an item of lore from the dominant culture and uses it in its own way and for its own purposes. In this respect, the Reggie Jackson urban legend among the Mennonites offers a case study parallel to that of the Vanishing Hitchhiker legend among the Mormons, which was well documented and analyzed by William A. Wilson in 1975.[6]

The Mennonite use of the Reggie Jackson legend not only refashions the story with details of Mennonite culture, as one might expect, but it also reveals an effective story-transmission network within the denomination in North America and suggests some interesting points about recent Mennonite sociology and psychology that help account for Mennonites' enthusiastic belief in and transmission of the story. Finally, it also stimulates some long thoughts about a possibly ingrained Mennonite preference for legend, as opposed to tale, in traditional narrative genres.

Mennonite Versions of the Story

The widest-known Mennonite version of the story appeared in the July 26, 1982, issue of *The Mennonite Reporter*, a biweekly inter-Mennonite publication distributed mainly in Canada. Apart from the ethnic identity given to the women, this version follows the main outline of the story as it was also told by non-Mennonite Americans:

What's your version? The story is being told of three Mennonite women from Lancaster, Pennsylvania, who made a visit to New York City. Before leaving on their trip they were advised by their husbands and friends to stick together and to be wary of strangers.

According to reports, the women stepped into an elevator to get to a restaurant in a city high rise. Just as the elevator doors were about to close, a man and his dog entered the elevator. The man said, "Sit!" And the three women promptly sat down. So goes the story.

The man assured the women that he had been speaking to his dog. They proceeded to the restaurant.

After the meal, when the women were ready to pay their bill, they found out that it had been picked up by the man they had met in the elevator—Reggie Jackson, they were told.

This story has appeared in a number of places, with a number of variations. According to our sources, the persons telling this story claim it is true. However, the storytellers do not personally know the people involved. They only know of someone (usually a friend or relative) who knows.

Have you heard the same story? What is the version that you have heard? Write to: Mennonite stories, c/o *Mennonite Reporter*, Waterloo, Ontario N2L 3G6.

The request elicited few responses and the paper printed only one, on August 23, before the editor, citing Jan Brunvand, exposed the story as untrue on September 20, 1982. Shortly after that, Mennonite interest in the story died.

My own collection of oral and written versions of the urban legend was made during August and September of l982—immediately after my return from a year in England—when the life of the legend had almost run its course. Most of my informants were from the Goshen College community in Indiana, which makes the results seem geographically limited until one recalls that Goshen is an important center of American Mennonitism. A Mennonite college, mental health center, retirement center, and mutual insurance company are located there and the community is less than ten miles from Elkhart, Indiana, where a Mennonite seminary and some administrative offices of the Mennonite Church are located. Many Mennonites of both Elkhart and Goshen have roots in other Mennonite communities throughout North America, and travel back and forth between them is extensive. My collection of texts includes thirty-seven full oral and written versions, many fragmentary reports, and extensive interviews and correspondence with informants who were influential in disseminating the legend among the Mennonites.

From that collection, a medium-length version told by a well-educated Goshen woman in her sixties is a good example of an oral telling of the legend:

> It's not often that I remember stories, because I'm not a great storyteller as you well know. But this one seemed to— maybe it's because I'm from Pennsylvania and I grew up knowing Mennonite women in black bonnets that this story had some special interest for me. But I remember, as he told the story, that there were four Mennonite women from Lancaster, Pennsylvania, who went to New York at the invitation of their husbands, for a special lark.
>
> And of course, before they went, they were well indoctrinated with all the rules of going to the city, because these were rural women. And they were told to be sure to guard their purses. There're a lot of pickpockets in New York. Be sure to stay out of the alleys, and be sure not to go out at night to dangerous places.
>
> But the women thought certainly as a special treat they could have a dinner at a very nice restaurant on one of the top floors of the building so they could overlook the city and see the lights.
>
> So they got into the elevator and felt quite safe because they were alone in the elevator. But of course the elevator stopped. And a black man and a dog got into the elevator. And they were going on their way up to the fourteenth or fifteenth floor when the man suddenly said, "Sit!" And the four women obediently fell to the floor. . . .

And the man was so embarrassed, and he said, "Oh, I beg your pardon. I was speaking to my dog." And, of course, I'm sure they were embarrassed, too. So they got out of the elevator and went and had their dinner. Then they came to the desk to pay their bill and the person at the desk said, "Well, your bill has already been paid by your benefactor." And when they gasped, the cashier said, "The black man on the elevator was Reggie Jackson." Now that's all I remember of the story.[7]

The informant first heard the story at a dinner party in her home, attended by other Mennonite couples in their sixties. It is her favorite story. She would rather tell it than any other.

Although variant details from other tellings will be mentioned and discussed later in this essay, hers is a typical example of the story that, in its heyday, circulated among Mennonites of Indiana, Ohio, Illinois, Michigan. Pennsylvania, Virginia, New York, Iowa, North Dakota, Idaho, Florida, California, Missouri, Oregon, and at least the province of Ontario in Canada. I heard it for the first time in Sheffield, England, when American Mennonite friends working in Birmingham visited us in April and told us the latest news from Elkhart County.

The story was usually attached to some women in the next town, adjacent state, or neighboring church—often somewhere east of the speaker's home. Some told it about the wife of a Mennonite pastor in the Bronx; others about the wife of a Mennonite pastor in Washington, D.C.; still others, about Esther Diener, wife of a Mennonite pastor in Pettisville, Ohio. In becoming thus attached to well-known women, the urban legend behaved as legends normally do: it settled on the most prominent mark or person on the horizon. That principle of folklore prevailed here despite the logical contradiction that the women named above are more city-wise than the typical Mennonite woman and would probably not in real life react in such a timorous way to the black man and his dog.

The Legend's Effect on One Mennonite Community

This association of legend with specific women was no academic or laughing matter for two of the women. In fact, it had real-life consequences, a kind of mixed blessing, for Esther Diener and her community. Her experience serves as a good case study in the way an urban legend can affect an individual's life as well as stimulate other related folk activities.

Esther Diener, wife of the pastor of West Clinton Mennonite Church, was owner and manager of Das Essen Haus, located near Pettisville in the heart of a community of about 3,000 Mennonites in Northwestern Ohio. Her restaurant served excellent food at reasonable prices in a homey atmosphere—breakfast, lunch, and dinner for the general public as well as catered meals for large groups upstairs in The Attic.

One fateful morning in April 1982, her husband Edward told the elevator story about some women from Pennsylvania to friends and customers gathered around the breakfast "round table" in the restaurant. Within several days, Mrs. Diener's friends began asking her about her encounter with Reggie Jackson in New York City. Despite her denials, the story continued to grow and spread, in this basic form, as told by Mrs. Diener herself on October 7, 1982:

> Two of my sisters or two of my friends—that varies; sometimes it's my sisters, sometimes it's my friends—went with me to New York. Our husbands had told us to be very, very careful—that [we were] liable to get nabbed. And he didn't want us to go alone but finally consented that we could go alone. And he had told us not to ride subways, to always take taxis. When we got on the elevator, take the express elevator that went clear up.
>
> It was our last night in New York and we had made the grade and hadn't had any problems at all, so we decided to go to a musical. And we came back from the musical and in the hotel where we stayed, on the top floor was a restaurant. And so we decided on this last night to go to the top floor to

Esther Diener standing outside her restaurant, The Essen Haus, Pettisville, Ohio. In Mennonite lore of Northwestern Ohio, Esther was one of the women who shared an elevator with Reggie Jackson in New York City.

the restaurant. So we got on the express elevator and were just ready to close the door. The door had already started going closed when a great big black man came and shoved the door open and had a big dog, and got on the elevator facing the door.

And after the elevator started to go, he said, "Sit." And then we were scared and we sat. And [according to] the story around here, nothing else was communicated between the two of us.

And then we went to the restaurant and were very scared. It was a great big restaurant. And we ordered our meal. And when we were all done eating the waitress did not bring our ticket. And when we asked for it she said, "No, it's already been paid. Your friend paid it." And we said, "We didn't know anyone in New York. What do you mean?" And she pointed way over in the other corner and said, "Well that, that black man over there paid your ticket." And we said, "Well, we don't even know who he is." And of course we were very scared. And she said, "Well, that's Reggie Jackson. Everybody knows him." And we said, "Well, why would he be paying *our* ticket?" And she said, "I don't know. Something about he embarrassed you, and so he wanted to make it up to you. But that's the kind of guy he is. He, he just does good things for people." So that's the version.

The effect of the story climaxed in July. Following a fifteen-minute denial of its truth by Mrs. Diener to a prominent businessman, he suddenly looked at her and said: "I thought you were a businesswoman, Mrs. Diener. If you're any kind of a decent businesswoman, you'll get some mileage out of this story." This resulted in a kind of folk festival—a "Reggie Jackson Special" day for Das Essen Haus on July 28-29, well advertised from four weeks in advance in the weekly newspaper

This advertisement appeared in *The Archbold* (Ohio) *Buckeye*, promoting Esther Diener's hog roast that commemorated her legendary encounter with Reggie Jackson in New York City.

The Archbold Buckeye.[8] The "special" consisted of a hog roast served under a tent adjacent to the restaurant proper. Five pigs were prepared, and entertainment was provided by a female vocalist-guitarist, and by the Fun Band from Swanton, Ohio, made up of instrumentalists seventy-five years and older who played on homemade and conventional instruments. The climax of the affair was the serving of a big cake decorated with the image of Reggie Jackson, out of whose mouth came the command, "Sit!" The event was a popular success, although not as big as Mrs. Diener had expected.

Such public purgation did not dispel the rumor of Mrs. Diener's association with the story. Instead, the attendant newspaper publicity apparently encouraged some doubting members of the community to assume that the Reggie Jackie social was intended to celebrate her encounter with Reggie Jackson, rather than to deny it as a rumor. Some even expected him to make an appearance at the event. In any case, for over a month following, hundreds of her customers—including non-Mennonites from Bryan, Defiance, and Toledo, Ohio—continued to ask her, in all seriousness, to tell about her memorable visit to New York City. This intense experience with the legend has made Mrs. Diener speculative: "I guess I have wondered, of all the stories that are available, why this—maybe I just thought this particular one took a bigger round and everybody talked about it more. It's an interesting study to me, too, in human nature."

One Mennonite Transmission Network

The story reached Pettisville, Ohio, and other Mennonite communities quickly, bearing the hallmark of truth because it traveled through an interlocking network of boards, conferences, and seminars in the Mennonite Church.

Although a few Mennonites claim to have heard a non-Mennonite version of the story years ago, and a few also had heard a Mennonite version of it earlier than 1982, the crucial telling of the story apparently occurred at the March 1982 meeting of the Mennonite Board of Congregational Ministries (henceforth MBCM) at Greencroft Center in Elkhart, Indiana. At that time, a Mennonite pastor from the Bronx used the story to illustrate the point of his devotional meditation for the group. His story, told as true, involved three non-Mennonite friends of colleagues of his wife, who is a psychologist in a public school district near New York City and who had first told him the story.

His hearers were eight directors of the Board, hailing from Kitchener, Ontario; Lancaster, Pennsylvania; Goshen, Indiana; Morton, Illinois; Harrisonville, Missouri; Eugene, Oregon; and Los Angeles, California. These directors returned to their far-flung homes and told the story in informal and formal settings, including Sunday morning meetings and ministerial associations.

The experience of the secretary of MBCM may serve as an example of how MBCM members helped spread the story, although his case is more dramatic than most because of the extensive traveling and speaking that he does throughout the denomination. A day after the board meeting he told the story during "sharing" time in his home congregation, thus establishing the conduit through which the story reached me in England. Ten days after the board meeting he told it at the Associated Mennonite Biblical Seminary in Elkhart, Indiana, at a seminar on Christian education attended by (Old) and General Conference Mennonites from places such as Newton, Kansas; Scottdale, Pennsylvania; Harrisonburg, Virgina; and Winnipeg, Manitoba—which must have further stimulated the spread of the story among American Mennonites. On May 1, 1982, he told the story during a report to a meeting of the Franconia (Pennsylvania) Mennonite Conference. In addition, he told it in many informal settings. "I tell it every chance I get," he says. "I think it's a funny story."

In all of these tellings he faithfully reported the story as having happened to friends of the pastor's wife in New York City. Yet by the time the MBCM reconvened in June, the story had been variously attached to three Mennonite women in Lancaster County, to the New York pastor's sister-in-law, to his mother, and even to his grandmother, who had died about twenty years earlier. But most usually the story was attached to his wife.

Through a similar network the story reached the Dieners' community in Fulton County, Ohio. Mr. Diener heard it at a meeting of the bishops and overseers of the Ohio Mennonite Conference in April, told there by the Ohio Conference minister, who had heard it earlier at a meeting of another Mennonite board. As has already been noted, Diener told it in his wife's restaurant about Pennsylvania Mennonite women. Another Archbold pastor who had also attended the overseers' meeting told the story to the Archbold ministerial association, whence it must also have spread into non-Mennonite groups.

Such transmission is impressive, both because of the Mennonite storytelling network it reveals and the authoritative stamp that this network gave the story.

Apparently the interlocking administrative network of boards and institutions serves not only to facilitate the official business of the church but also to spread throughout the constituency the best stories currently making the rounds. As one member of the MBCM said, "Some of the greatest storytellers are the guys on these boards." In fact, time for storytelling is sometimes built into official meetings, as was the case at the Christian education seminar when the Reggie Jackson story emerged during a half-hour period specifically set aside for storytelling. Mennonites who complain of increased bureaucracy of the Mennonite Church might be pleased with the efficiency of the "trickle-down" system as they contemplate the rapid, wide spread of the Reggie Jackson story through the official church network. They might well wonder, however, why official church news and business does not travel equally well through those same networks!

Transmitted as it was—unofficially through the official church networks—the story obviously gained credibility through the quality of the tellers and situations in which the story was told. The integrity context was high. At least in its earliest tellings the story gained credence through the aura of responsible Mennonitism borne by board members as well as through the church assemblies at which the story was told. Unlike the Vanishing Hitchhiker story among the Mormons, which began with grassroots telling and was actively combated by officials of the church, the Reggie Jackson story began with Mennonite church officials and then spread easily among the laity. This difference in transmission between Mormon and Mennonite legendry is ironic, in light of the hierarchical nature of the Mormon Church and the much more informal nature of Mennonite fellowship.

Mennonites' belief in the story because of the teller's integrity created some difficult situations, particularly for those church leaders most instrumental in its spread. Once other media began reporting the story with non-Mennonite principals, and once the presumed Mennonite principals of the story began denying it, the reputations of early tellers were at stake. Memos were sent back and forth between members of the chain of transmission, often bearing photocopies of printed references to the legend and queries such as one addressed to the New York pastor: "Are you sure about your sources?" The situation produced monumental embarrassment for him and his wife, who could be most easily "blamed" for starting the story but who had never told it about Mennonite women. It has made that pastor "almost afraid to tell another story" lest his personal "integrity" be questioned again.

Like other tellers of contemporary legends, an impressive number of Mennonite informants believed the story not so much because they trusted the persons who told it to them but because they knew the women the story was about. One informant believed the story because her niece works for the Archbold woman to whom it (presumably) happened. Another believed it because her friend's granddaughter has a friend whose mother was one of the women involved. The comment of one believer, "I know the people. It has to be true," epitomizes this point.

The Meaning of the Legend for Mennonites

Although the pattern of dissemination described above explains how the story made the rounds, the important question is why this particular legend was so readily accepted by Mennonites. Pointing to its inherently Mennonite appeal, one fine raconteur said that the story simply "sounds better" with Mennonites in it, as opposed, for instance, to "Presbyterians from downtown Goshen." Another reported how a Methodist friend of hers enjoyed the story so much "because he knows the Mennonites, you know."

What makes the Reggie Jackson story into a truly Mennonite urban legend? To answer this question, we must consider the correspondences between the legend and Mennonite culture, in the same way that William A. Wilson has considered the relationship between the Vanishing Hitchhiker and Mormon culture. As he points out, the Vanishing Hitchhiker story was almost ready-made for adaptation and adoption by the Mormons because of their long-standing narrative tradition of the three Nephites, or angels, that appear to faithful Mormons, bearing prophecies of the future. The ghostly rider in the automobile easily became a Mormon spiritual visitor; the conversation easily turned into the conventional admonition to store up goods for the future years of want.[9]

If we consider Mennonite culture in the same way, we may assume that Mennonites will usually *not* be expected to tell with conviction the Vanishing Hitchhiker tale, because Mennonites have traditionally been quite unsupernatural in their everyday outlook.[10] The same type of elimination can be tentatively applied to other urban legends that vie for Mennonite attention. For instance, my larger collection of Mennonite folk narratives includes Mennonite accounts of the disappearing grandmother, the urine in the whiskey bottle, the keys in the stolen handbag, and the double accident on the ski slope.[11] All were told concurrently with the Reggie Jackson story but none were disseminated widely among Mennonites. Why not? Perhaps the ski slope story deals with a recreation too far removed from most

Mennonites' experience. Certainly the ski slope and urine stories are too vulgar to be told in solemn assemblies. Perhaps none lends itself to moral application in as many senses as the Reggie Jackson story does.

In puzzling through the possible "meanings" of the Reggie Jackson legend, we can gain some sense of its positive appeal for Mennonites from explicit comments of those who told the story in formal settings. For instance, in telling the story to the MBCM, the New York pastor gave it a theological interpretation in a short devotional, "The Identity of Jesus," based on the question posed by Jesus in Mark 8:27: "Who do men say that I am?" The pastor intended the story of Reggie Jackson to show how the identity one assigns to a person affects one's experience with him: expecting evil things from a black man, the women responded to him wrongly until they finally experienced his true, benevolent nature. So it is also with the Christian and Jesus. Predisposed to see Jesus as a conservative (or radical, or anti-feminist), Christians must reorient themselves when they come within the presence of Christ himself. According to the pastor, he intended the story as an a illustration, not as a "joke." Nor did his hearers find it funny, he says.

This stipulated meaning for the story certainly did not stick with the story for long, although apparently when it was told in formal church contexts some kind of moral or theological application was often made. One line that such interpretations probably followed is pointed to by one of the original hearers of the MBCM version. She likes the "subtle reminder that is in it of the power of generous and forgiving actions." Reggie Jackson, slugger, might be surprised to learn that, in the Mennonite tradition, he is a kind of Christ-figure.

Most Mennonite tellers, of course, need not and do not bring to conscious awareness the reasons for the appeal of the story to them. However, we can arrive at some such meanings indirectly, by considering theological, sociological, and psychological biases of contemporary Mennonites and the way the Reggie Jackson story builds on and clarifies them.

In short, we can relate the deep seated fears and aspirations of Mennonites to this particular urban legend in the same way that sociologist Gary Alan Fine has connected pervasive qualities of modern American mass culture with urban legendry.[12] Scattered comments on the story by Mennonites involved in its spread give guideposts for such thinking and help elevate speculation into actuality. They point to four main topics of appeal embodied in the story: urbanization, feminism, nonconformity, and racism.

Urbanizaton

When the MBCM secretary told the story to the Franconia Conference meeting, he connected it to a previous speaker's comments on common fears of the city. The New York pastor indirectly perceives the same connection when he observes that rural Mennonites find the story funnier than do urban Mennonites.

The most basic motif of the story is indeed the movement by Mennonites from the hinterlands to the big bad city. In miniature, the principals enact the experience that Mennonites have faced during their recent years in America and that they will increasingly face in the future: leaving the countryside and finding a way to cope with city living. Although the popular American imagination sees Mennonites as farming people, the demographic facts are otherwise. In the sociological survey of various Mennonite groups published by J. Howard Kauffman and Leland J. Harder in 1975, statistics showed that only thirty-eight percent of Mennonites lived on farms of three acres or more. The rest lived near or in small towns and cities (but with only twelve percent, however, living in cities with a population of 25,000 or over).[13] True, this distribution still makes Mennonites more rural than the rest of the American population, but the fact remains that a formerly rural people have rapidly given up farming as an occupation and moved to urban settings and occupations.

As the statistics indicate, the movement into the really big cities has not yet been extensive, although Mennonites have tried to establish missions in big cities since early in the century. However, as a recent documentation of the Chicago Mennonite missions has shown,[14] that movement has not been very successful. Mennonites have long felt called to the city as a mission field, but few have been able to cope successfully with their own move from rural environs to urban, and from an ethnically uniform, comfortable enclave to an ethnically diverse setting in the city.

The Reggie Jackson story depicts the worst fears of innocents abroad in the city, yet also shows their fondest hopes realized. To some extent, the story does show Mennonites that they can leave their homes in the countryside and find a welcome and happy experience in the city. Even so, the scope of the story limits the amount of assurance that can be derived from it. Limited as it is to the interior of the hotel, the Mennonites' contact with real city life is only superficial and even artificial. In their top floor restaurant, they only survey the city; they do not truly enter it. And they are, after all, only visitors to the city, not would-be dwellers in it. Their tentative contact with the city may mirror Mennonites' limited desire to become truly urbanized, better than most Mennonites would consciously admit.

Feminism

The story is a "put-down of women," says one elderly man with a feminist conscience. Now that he knows the story is not true, he tells it about some Mennonite "couples" rather than "three Mennonite women."[15] His conscious re-interpretation of the story makes explicit some latent misogynist meanings—Mennonite style—in the story.

The basic story has as one of its chief motifs the ridiculous fears and behaviors of the women involved. The narrative typically begins with the unliberated women contrasted, unfavorably, with their husbands. In many versions, the women accompany their husbands to the city where the men—frequently Mennonite pastors—are attending a church conference. The women have never been to New York City before; their husbands have. Just like little children, they need to be given condescendingly strict instructions—by their husbands—on how to behave in a new situation. Their husbands have a purpose in going to the city; the women have none, except to eat dinner or, more rarely, to go shopping (or, still more rarely, to go to a play or musical). Come nighttime, they obey their husbands' cautions to the letter, showing little sense of imagination or adventure.

Their sitting in the elevator is the climax of the implied ridicule, although that is increased by their not recognizing Reggie Jackson, even after the personal encounter is over. Finally, the women are so "dense" that they tell the story to other people after it is over. "I would have made a pact with the other two never to let a story like that get out," one female teller said.

These misogynistic elements are increased by a Mennonite milieu and by the details of traditional Mennonite culture that that milieu often supplies for the story. Whereas non-Mennonite versions typically rationalize the timidity of the women by describing them as elderly people,[16] Mennonite versions often account for the comic behavior by invoking Mennonite costume conventions and the sociological attitudes that these costumes carry with them.

When the women are not given individual names, they are most often described as "very conservative ladies" from Lancaster County, Pennsylvania, where the traditional "plain garb" was best preserved among Mennonite women in 1982. They are the kind of women who wear "black bonnets," "covering strings," "cape dresses and all that." "I can just visualize it, can't you?" says one informant. In some communities these bonnets, coverings, strings, and cape dresses were elements of regulation costume for women as prescribed by male leaders of the church.[17] Although all were part of the "plain" costume intended to preserve the ideal of modesty in adornment—particularly the cape dresses—the bonnet, covering, and covering strings are directly associated with the subordinate position of women in traditional Mennonite culture, since they are one way that Mennonites fulfill literally the admonition of Paul in 1 Corinthians 11:3-6:

> The head of every man is Christ, the head of a woman is her husband, and the head of Christ is God. Any man who prays or prophesies with his head covered dishonors his head, but any woman who prays or prophesies with her head unveiled dishonors her head. It is the same as if her head were shaven. For if a woman will not veil herself, then she should cut off her hair; but if it is disgraceful for a woman to be shorn or shaven, let her wear a veil.

Since in many locales the covering and bonnet were prescribed as everyday regulation attire for all activities—not only prayer—they have, in effect, become symbols of Mennonite women's subordination to men. It is this sense of female diminishment, then, that explains one informant's description of them as "three little Mennonite women" and another's as "three little timid Lancaster County women, cowering." "Little" here has figurative meaning, created by the garb that diminishes womanhood. It makes them frail and vulnerable in Mennonite versions of the story and is therefore the counterpart of the advanced age of the "elderly" women in mainstream American versions of the legend.

Although relatively few Mennonite women in other parts of North America still wear the covering, memories of it were still close enough and the status of women was still ambiguous enough to enable the story to cut near to the sexual-identity bone in 1982. The circulation of the story at that time, in fact, came midway between the Mennonite General Assembly meetings at Bowling Green, Ohio, in 1981, and at Bethlehem, Pennsylvania, in 1983, at both of which sessions the question of the role of women in the church—particularly in leadership roles, such as ordained minister—was in dispute. The time was ripe in 1982 for a derogatory story about Mennonite women. Most of my versions, in fact, came from the Goshen College community, where the role of women was a lively topic for discussion during the 1981-82 academic year. The feminist forces on campus were so vocal and assertive at that time that many men felt that the atmosphere precluded rational discourse on the issue—and certainly forbade even slightly derogatory comments about women. In such a situation, the "true" story of three Mennonite women in New York City could serve as the perfect escape valve. It could be told with a clean conscience because it had actually happened; it could be told to inject—even if indirectly and unconsciously— a nay-saying into the feminist rhetoric that dominated the community's discussion and feelings.

Oddly enough, though, the story was apparently told as often, as enthusiastically and as effectively by women as by men—sometimes even by those who were leading the feminist cause. One such woman, in fact, thought that the story was best told with a cut-off at the point where the women sat in the elevator. Such an ending would include no denouement to clarify or diplomatically resolve the situation; it would leave Mennonite women cruelly exposed. One even younger feminist enjoyed telling this story so much that, as one observer recorded her performance, she "squats on the floor and rolls her eyes meekly" and then proceeds to "really getting into the story— demonstrates their squat several times."[18]

Of course, one reason Mennonite feminists could endorse the story is that it depicts precisely what they say has been wrong with Mennonite women in the past. They have been excessively "submissive" and "obedient." Feminists, then, told the story to discredit the "little Mennonite women" from Pennsylvania. Men told it, whether consciously or unselfconsciously, as their oblique, more general contribution to the debate on feminism.

Nonconformity

The publicity given the Reggie Jackson story in *The Mennonite Reporter* elicited an enlightened protest from one correspondent: "Why do Mennonites have a need to develop a mythology of association with the high and mighty—or at least the well-known?"[19] Indeed, in some Mennonite versions of the legend, the Mennonite women "associate" very closely with Reggie Jackie. Whereas in most they simply recognize him across the room of diners, in other versions he waves to them, they visit with him at his table, or Reggie even takes them out to dinner instead. Although the correspondent refers to no other stories that belong to this denominational "mythology" of social aspirations, he might have referred to Mennonite encounters with Stonewall Jackson, Abraham Lincoln, and Samuel Colt, all of which have been used to regale Mennonite audiences.[20]

Implicit in the correspondent's objection is his endorsement of the traditional Mennonite doctrine of nonconformity, based on the admonition, "And be not conformed to this world" (Rom. 12:2).[21] Although at its most profound level the doctrine assumes a nonresistant way of life, in a more tangible sense it has actually led to Mennonites living physically "separate" from other groups of people. At times this has meant, as with the Amish, a slowness in embracing technological innovations and also a visual separateness through distinctive garb.

Mennonite nonconformity is obviously present in the versions of the story referred to thus far, most obviously in the special clothing of the women, as discussed above. In one striking version, it is also present in a unique recognition scene, where—according to a middle-aged woman from Goshen—the dining women receive the note from Jackson along with a bottle of wine:

> They were eating their meal, and a bottle of wine was put on their table by the waiter. And they said, "Well, there must be some mistake." He said, "No. There's a card here. It says, 'For you.'" "Yes, but we don't drink any wine. We didn't order this." He said, "But it says, 'For you.'" And so they opened the card, and here it said, "You've made my day. Reggie Jackson."

Here the women's separation from the world is illustrated by their abstinence from alcoholic beverages, which has been a rather distinctive Mennonite cultural trait since Prohibition.

In a more general sense, nonconformity is also present in the women's ignorance of city ways, and perhaps even in the husbands' obsession with the evil in the city. What is merely provincial naiveté in most American tellings of the story becomes more culturally and doctrinally charged with meaning in Mennonite versions of the story, since both Mennonite men and their wives apparently find it hard to accommodate their separate, nonconformed spirit and lives to the city, where fallen worldliness traditionally resides.

The most obvious evidence of Mennonite nonconformity in the story lies in the women's failing to recognize Reggie Jackson—first in the elevator when he enters, later in the restaurant when they see him again and, finally, even when the cashier tells them his name. "That type of woman [i.e., conservative] probably would not recognize Reggie Jackson," says one informant.[22]

A version from a college-age Goshen woman illustrates this narrative feature:

> And the waitress said, "Well, somebody else has already taken care of [the bill]. It's been paid." And they—you know, they were really bewildered, and, well, she said, "It's that gentleman sitting over there." And they turned around and it was the black man that was in the elevator, sitting there. And he looked like he was eating something or just finished or something. And they were, you know, they just didn't know what to do! And they said, "Well, we don't know him," and all this. And she said, "You don't know who he is?" And she said, "Well, that's Reggie Jackson." And the Mennonite women weren't quite sure exactly who Reggie Jackson was. But then one of them kind of thought, "Oh, yeah, that, that name. I think my husband said he was a famous sports person or something." And so they accepted the check and went home.

Whereas in the typical American version the mere naming of "Reggie Jackson" is a punch line that creates recognition and concludes the telling, in the many Mennonite versions that assume the isolation of the women from "worldly" culture, the narrative often dwindles out with an anti-climax of explanation and confused speculation on Jackson's actual identity.

Whether or not the Mennonite story involves recognition of or contact with Reggie Jackson by the women, *The Mennonite Reporter* correspondent rightly identifies the appeal that this exposure to—and acceptance by—an American superstar has for a people, who, while paying lip service to nonconformity to the world, have gradually abandoned their signs of physical distinctiveness and are entering the mainstream of American occupations, recreations, and cultural interest. This appeal of the story might satisfy the query, quoted earlier, as to why any Mennonite women would be so stupid as to repeat an embarrassing story once they returned to their husbands or to their homes. One possibility is that their elation from meeting, recognizing, and being recognized by a popular American idol would win over their personal pride. True, such meeting with the great probably also accounts for the story's popularity with the American public in general. But the appeal of the story to Mennonites on this basis may have been even greater, since the recognition is harder won by Mennonites, and their acceptance is psychologically more latent with cultural and theological implications.

In at least two Mennonite communities such contact with Reggie Jackson had existential, not merely theoretical, implications. For instance, one of the early tellers of the story, an MBCM member from Missouri, enjoyed telling the story to his home congregation because one member actually boarded and trained horses for Reggie Jackson, who had even eaten with them in their home on one occasion. The story was well received by his parishioners and thoroughly believed by them because they "know Reggie as a gracious man."

The Dieners in Pettisville, Ohio, came closest to actual contact with Reggie Jackson as the result of the legend's spread. After having advertised the special day at the restaurant, Mrs. Diener had questions about the legality of exploiting the name of a famous person for a business enterprise. So she called Reggie Jackson and talked with his agent, who did not deny the truth of the story and finally agreed that she could use his employer's name. "Go right ahead and have your fun," he said. "Reggie said it's perfectly all right. Just don't do it again." Mrs. Diener assumes that the voice she heard in the background during the telephone conversation was that of Reggie Jackson himself.

The temptation toward worldliness created a little anguish for the Dieners as they planned the special day. One nagging doubt of theirs was whether they should capitalize on the story and Reggie Jackson's fame—"with our kind of restaurant," as they put it. In other words, should a home-style restaurant operated by Mennonites in a predominantly Mennonite community identify itself with American show business techniques and superstars from the world of American entertainment? Like their fellow Mennonites who relished the story in retelling it, the Dieners resolved their dilemma and conformed.

Racism

"That's a racist story," said one well-educated Mennonite upon hearing the story for the first time. Indeed, as Reggie Jackson and his dog face the timorous women in the elevator, all he needs is a whip in his hand to recreate the worst fears of Caucasians, based on stereotypical notions of what would happen if blacks ever gained power in the United States. However, this knee-jerk interpretation of the story is only half correct, since the wish-fulfillment ending of the story, as usually told by Mennonites, is almost always to the black man's credit. The story must be grounded in white Mennonites' fears of black people, but it almost invariably vindicates their faith in the good will of black people. As such, it serves as a good image of where American Mennonites were in 1982 regarding race relations.

The testimony of African-American Mennonites also speaks

to the non-racist impact of the story. When the MBCM secretary prepared to tell the story at the Franconia Conference meeting, in the presence of several African-American Mennonites from Philadelphia, he first tried out the story on one of them in order to test his reactions. The African-American leader, who had already heard and enjoyed it, encouraged him to tell it. From his point of view, it was a story illustrating the superiority of the black man to the white women.

Indeed, few Mennonite tellings included details that would bring out the most racist tendencies within the tradition of this particular urban legend. No Mennonite version in my collection, for instance, tells the story about Larry Holmes, the African-American boxer of somewhat menacing mien[23]; all are about the lighter-skinned, kindly-looking Reggie Jackson. One version does describe the Doberman pinscher as "straining at the leash." Another has Reggie tell his (white) dog, "Sit! you white bitch!" Still others have Reggie laugh at the squatting women or tell them, disgustedly, "I meant the dog!" But many, many more versions depict Reggie Jackson as genuinely embarrassed by the grief he had caused the women. According to one teller, he was more embarrassed than the women were. Some say he was even "horrified" by what he had done. In addition, only a rare few have Reggie's note reading, "Thanks, ladies! You've made my day." In that version, Reggie is a cad who gives the dinner to the women out of appreciation for the laugh they gave him. Most Mennonite versions refer to a note that says, "With apologies for frightening you in the elevator."

One female teller was "touched" by the story; she likes it because the "black man paid the bill. He's a gentleman." For Mrs. Diener, "That's the kind of guy he is. He, he just does good things for people." Some others who comment on the story go one step further and see in the Reggie Jackson of the legend the embodiment of all, or at least many other, black men. One is impressed that "a big urban black man" can be so generous and forgiving. Another points out that the story proves that "not all black males are to be feared. They may be the most gracious."

Lest this interpretation be regarded as too optimistic, too favorable a picture of Mennonites in a racially tense society, one should recall the statistics on Mennonite attitudes toward African-Americans contained in the Kauffman-Harder survey in 1975. Their investigation showed that (Old) Mennonites were less racially prejudiced than were other Mennonite groups and that Mennonites as a whole were less prejudiced than Catholics and other Protestant groups.[24]

The Reggie Jackson story, then, becomes an illustration of the statistical data. While Mennonites' deepest fears may match those of mainstream America, at least their conscious thinking and their unselfconscious storytelling do jibe. Neither percentages nor urban legends are the equivalent of social action, but both should give courage to Mennonites in the city—whether they go there to establish new churches, to establish professional careers or, as in the story, just for a visit.

Mennonites and Legends

In addition to its mode of transmission and its socio-psychological appeal, the Reggie Jackson story probably spread so rapidly among Mennonites because it belongs to a certain narrative genre—urban *legend*. If the definitive description of Mennonite storytelling is ever written, I predict that it will demonstrate a decided preference among Mennonites for the legend (i.e., the story told as true) as opposed to the folktale (i.e., the fictional narrative such as the joke, the tall tale, etc.). The Beachy Amish minister mentioned in chapter 1 as denying that he ever told a story that was not true, as well as the relationship of the Mennonite tricksters in chapter 3 to Matthew 5:34-37, "Let your communication be Yea, yea; Nay, nay," support this point.

In regard to the relationship between word and act, Kermit Eby, a leader in the Church of the Brethren, recognized the moral connection between a life of integrity and the tradition of non-swearing of the oath when he referred to the Mennonite and Church of the Brethren "emphasis on integrity [and] their refusal of the oath. These two positions are not unrelated."[25]

An overtly perceivable honesty in speaking and physical appearance are even two ethnic traits that some Mennonites cited when asked, "How do you know a Mennonite when you see one?"[26]

> If that person is able to look at me in a candid, friendly way (17). . . . I'd eliminate those that are loud and noisy . . . I'd look for a certain innocence. It's been said that Mennonites look honest. (18) . . . Mennonites have that overt honesty about them. They tend to be gullible. Again, it's the overt honesty factor; people are to be believed for what they say (14).

J. C. Wenger, noted Mennonite historian and raconteur, linked such observations to Mennonite storytelling when he, too, noted a preference for the story told as true. "We have been a very uncritical people," he observed. "If somebody that you know is an honest man tells [a story], it must be true."[27]

Legend-telling, then, is both a moral imperative and an ingrained tendency in the ethnic subconsciousness of Mennonites.[28] Historically, the legends that have been most important in Mennonite culture are the "saints' lives" that have found their way into *Martyrs Mirror,* the compendium of accounts of sixteenth- and seventeenth-century Anabaptist martyrs. The contemporary equivalents are stories of more recent spiritual heroism, as in *The Path of Most Resistance*, which honors Mennonite draft-resisters during the Vietnam war.[29] Yet such stories, whether of ancient or contemporary Mennonite heroic "martyrs," are the *official* legendry of the church, printed in books and told in formal, large-group gatherings but not repeated in informal conversation, in the manner of *unofficial* or "folk" culture.[30]

The truly living tradition of Mennonite folk legend is what folklorists call the *anecdote*—that is, the short *personal legend* told as true about a well-known person in the community, whether that be the local, national, or worldwide Mennonite community.[31]

Such stories about H. S. Bender, Orie O. Miller, John Howard Yoder, C. F. Derstine—usually satirical, seldom faith-building—by far predominate in my large collection of Mennonite narratives. These stories, which are sometimes adaptations of traditional narratives, derive their ethnic appeal from being attached to a well-known person, which means that the gossipy "Mennonite game" becomes transformed into semi-fictional narrative form.

My collecting of oral texts shows that the urban legend per se does not often become adapted to the Mennonite narrative tradition, which is what makes the Reggie Jackson story of particular interest. Something special contributed to its acceptance by Mennonites. That apparently was just the right combination of narrative content, personalized characters, socio-psychological appeal, an optimum introduction to the Mennonite transmission network—and the assurance from honest people that it was indeed a "true" story.

CPS Protest Songs

with Vincent S. Beck and Charlotte Hertzler Croyle

The protest songs in this essay were sung by the "bad boys" in Civilian Public Service (CPS) camps in Mancos, Colorado, and Lapine (Wickiup), Oregon, during World War II.

Since they were sung in the presence of Mennonite conscientious objectors (COs) and were sometimes sung by Mennonite COs themselves, the songs contribute additional evidence to recent discussions of how nonresistant Mennonite young men eventually moved from passive cooperation with the government toward outright resistance to government coercion, especially as embodied in the Selective Service system.

The songs were collected and sung by my brother Vincent S. Beck (1923-2003) of Archbold, Ohio. They became publicly known through the CPS oral history project sponsored by the Zion Mennonite Church of Archbold and carried out by Charlotte Hertzler Croyle, who originally worked with Vincent and his materials.

A description of the contexts in which the songs were originally sung will illuminate the personal and social meanings that they carry.

Vincent S. Beck

Civilian Public Service was a government program that provided alternate work assignments in the U.S. for conscientious objectors to military duty during World War II. The program served both religious and nonreligious objectors to war. From 1941 to 1946 about 150 "CPS camps" were scattered throughout the U.S., mainly in relatively isolated areas. The CPS camps for nonreligious objectors were administered by the Selective Service administration; those for religious objectors were sponsored and supervised mainly by civilians from the historic peace churches—Mennonites, Quakers, and Brethren. About 12,000 COs, including about 4,000 Mennonite and Amish men, performed work of "national importance," especially in conservation and mental health.

Mennonite men tended to work in the church-sponsored camps, although Vincent Beck and some others occasionally

Vincent S. Beck (1923-2003) in cowboy uniform during his Civilian Public Service in the San Joaquim Valley, California, in 1943.

worked with nonreligious objectors in the government-sponsored camps. The nonreligious objectors, who were often political leftists and sometimes refused to cooperate in the CPS camps, were the "bad boys." The Mennonite men and others who cooperated in their work assignments were the "good boys."[1]

When he was drafted in the spring of 1943, Vincent S. Beck left his home in Pettisville, Ohio, for the CPS camp in Grottoes, Virginia, administered by the Mennonite Church for young men from historic peace churches—Brethren, Friends, Mennonites. About two months later he was transferred to a similar camp, the North Fork Camp in the High Sierras near Fresno, California.

In October 1943, he moved to Mancos, Colorado, and in January 1944, to Lapine, Oregon. Both camps were administered by the Selective Service administration for men who were not affiliated with the historic peace churches. These were often the "bad boys" of CPS, who tended to cause trouble for camp administrators by refusing to cooperate. Peace church men could choose to be placed in those camps, however. Vincent volunteered for the Mancos camp and later accepted reassignment to the Lapine camp, in both cases because he wanted to work in as many different locations as possible during his CPS experience. At Mancos he helped build an earthen dam on the Mancos River and was on call to help fight forest fires. At Lapine he cut and bulldozed trees in an area that was later to become the bottom of a lake behind a dam. In February 1945, he moved to the unit operated by the Church of the Brethren at the veterans hospital in Lyons, New Jersey. Finally in late February of 1946 he spent seven weeks on the ship *Plymouth Victory*, which delivered 900 horses to war-ravaged Poland. Then he returned to Pettisville, where he soon began selling life insurance and gradually developed a general insurance agency, V.S. Beck Insurance Agency in Archbold, Ohio, from which he retired in 1985.

It is possible to identify several personal reasons why Vincent became a preserver of these unusual songs. First, he was a singer and guitar player, especially of country-western music.

He took his guitar along to CPS and played it for his own and his friends' recreation. He naturally paid more attention than others to the music that he encountered in CPS. Like other Mennonites at Mancos and Lapine, he joined in singing the songs when they were sung in the camp dining halls. Although he never led in their public singing, he did sing them by himself during personal time near his bunk.

Second, Vincent's own attitude toward his CPS experience was ambivalent. Although he always was a staunch conscientious objector to war—"There was no indecision on my part . . . about conscientious objection to war"—he shared some of the "bad boys" feelings about being coerced by the government into work without pay. Like them, he sometimes called CPS "Civilian Public Servitude" and referred to camp work as "involuntary servitude." These attitudes seem to have been influenced by his experience with the "bad boys" at Mancos and Lapine. Vincent says he entered CPS, like most other Mennonite young men, as a "nonresistant" Christian. However, he began to regard himself as a "nonviolent" Christian instead, largely because of his exposure to non-Mennonites and their more resistant stance to governmental coercion.

Also, upon returning from CPS Vincent felt betrayed by his church when he began to sell life insurance, which was at that time forbidden by the Mennonite Church—but which the Mennonite Church itself soon after began to sell, under the name of "survivors aid" through Mennonite Mutual Aid Association.

As an insurance agent in Archbold, Ohio, he was attacked from both sides—by ministers in the Mennonite Church that he had been faithful to during the war and by non-Mennonites in the community who painted one of his business signs yellow and threw a sack of manure through the door into his insurance office.

Perhaps the critical, even sometimes bitter tone and words of the songs express both his feelings of "involuntary servitude" during CPS and his continuing sense of unfair treatment by the Mennonite Church.

Three men standing outside the "Tobacco Road" barracks at CPS #111, Mancos, Colorado. The sign over the door says "Colonel Mac Welcome to Tobacco Road."

Mancos and Lapine Camps

Vincent acquired about half of the songs at Mancos and the other half at Lapine. They were composed and sung by essentially the same people at both places, since the CPSers at Lapine had been transferred there from Mancos. Usually they were sung in the dining hall prior to eating. Camp administrators never tried to stop the singing.

Vincent recalled the dramatic moment in the dining room at Lapine when "Old Man Olsen Had a Camp," printed below, was first sung. The camp was in transition from Mennonite- to government-run. The sixteen Mennonite men who had not yet been transferred out were at a table on one side of the mess hall;

the newly transferred non-Mennonite Mancos men were at another table; camp administrators were at a third in the front of the room.

The Mennonite men had earlier been given a printed set of songs and forewarned that they would be sung at mealtime. As Vincent put it, "The government men and the Mennonite campers were aghast when the Mancos Group boldly sang 'Old Man Olsen Had a Camp.'" Thus the "bad boys" from Mancos, during their first meal at Lapine, gave fair warning to their government bosses that they would be a non-cooperative lot.

Vincent described the Mancos men as "ready and willing to go to prison, men who were anti-war, anti-conscription, and anti-slavery, and didn't hesitate to let the government men know it." They were "individualistic and very intelligent" people, often coming from Yale, Harvard, and the University of Chicago—real "brains," as the song "Our Old and Dusty Loam" describes such troublemakers.

If they became too resistant at the special camps created for other than historic peace church objectors, the worst trouble-

Bull session at Mancos Camp. The sign in the background says, "Pretend you like it."

makers were sent to an isolated camp for offenders begun in Germfask, Michigan, by December 1944.

The names of the authors of a few of the songs have been preserved, although Vincent recalled little about them: J. F. Kendrick, Al Partridge, Dwight Riemann, Frank Hatfield. Hatfield, who wrote three of the songs, was an outspoken, smart university-trained New Englander.

For their first singings, all of the texts of the songs given below were presented to Vincent and others in printed form. They are grouped below according to topic, rather than the sequence of Vincent's typewritten collection.

Socialist Songs

Some of the "bad boys"—perhaps especially those more articulate ones from Yale, Harvard, and the University of Chicago—expressed somewhat socialist convictions through many of these songs. Vincent refers to some of these men as "anti-capitalists." Perhaps Melvin Gingerich, Mennonite historian, was thinking of the same people when he referred to the "radicalism produced by our contacts with pacifists."[2]

"Christians at War," written by J. F. Kendrick, was to be sung to the tune of "Onward, Christian Soldiers." In attributing war-making to the urge for profit, in indicting organized religion, in implying that preachers are pigs (line 6), and in its offensive rhetoric the song betrays its aggressively leftist political bias:

> Onward, Christian soldiers,
>   duty's way is plain;
> Slay your Christian neighbors,
>   or by them be slain.
> Pulpiteers are spouting
>   effervescent swill,
> God above is calling you
>   to rob and rape and kill.

All your acts are sanctified
    by the Lamb on high;
If you love the Holy Ghost,
    go murder, pray, and die.

Onward, Christian soldiers,
    rip and smite and tear;
Let the gentle Jesus
    bless your dynamite.
Splinter skulls with shrapnel,
    fertilize the sod;
Folks who do not speak your tongue
    deserve the curse of God.
Smash the doors of every home,
    pretty maidens seize;
Use your might and sacred right
    to treat them as you please.

Onward, Christian soldiers,
    eat and drink your fill.
Rob with bloody fingers,
    Christ OKs the bill.
Steal the farmer's savings,
    Take their grain and meat.
Even though the children starve,
    the Savior's bums must eat;
Burn the peasants' cottages,
    orphans leave bereft;
In Jehovah's holy name,
    wreak ruin right and left.

Onward, Christian soldiers,
    drench the land with gore,
Mercy is a weakness
    all the gods abhor;
Bayonet the babies,
    jab the mothers, too;

Hoist the cross of Calvary
　　　to hallow all you do.
File the bullets' noses flat,
　　　poison every well,
God decrees your enemies
　　　must all go plum to hell.

Onward, Christian soldiers,
　　　blighting all you meet,
Trampling human freedom
　　　under pious feet.
Praise the Lord whose dollar-sign,
　　　dupes his favored race;
Make the foreign trash respect
　　　your bullion brand of grace.
Trust in mock salvation,
　　　serve as pirates' tools,
History will say of you,
　　　"That pack of G . . . D fools."

"Money Patriots" also emphasizes the association between government power and moneyed interests. As Vincent explained it, the song reveals "the usual Fourth-of-July type of 'patriotic spouting' for what it is—money-grabbing and hypocritical expression of belief in Christianity and devotion to one's country." The words are to be sung to the tune of "Clementine":

Join the party that is ruling,
Give the boss what brains you've got.
Play the roosters be a booster,
And you'll be a patriot.

CHORUS:
O my country, O, my country,
How I love each blooming spot!
But ain't it funny how for money
One may be a patriot.

Go to church and talk like honey,
Kiss the flag and shout a lot,
That will make you for they'll take you
For a blooming patriot.

Boom your business, boom your business,
Brother love it matters not.
Use your gall, sir, do them all, sir,
Then you'll be a patriot.

If the "bad boys" could compose nasty songs, they did at
times also sing songs that offered a more positive description of
what they stood for. "My Country Is the World," to be sung to
the tune of "America," gives an attractive picture of a worldwide brotherhood that constitutes a secular, humanistic basis
for conscientious objection to war:

My country is the world,
My flag with stars impearled,
Fills all the skies.
All the round earth I claim,
Peoples of every name;
And all-inspiring fame,
My heart would prize.

And all men are my kin,
Since every man has been
Blood of my blood.
I glory in the grace
And strength of every race,
And joy in every trace
Of brotherhood.

Since this song refers neither to war-making nor to camp
life, it may have been composed and sung prior to any of the
men's being drafted.

At the other end of the continuum of socialist commitment

is "Solidarity Forever," which uses the Marxist motto of "solidarity" and even exhorts camp members to organize and strike. Substituting "workers" for "campers" in line 2 would make the song a rousing labor movement song. And, indeed, the song was written for the labor movement in 1915 by Ralph Chaplin, who in 1918 was sentenced to twenty years in prison for his activities on behalf of the Industrial Workers of the World (IWW).[3] "Campers" is substituted only one time for "workers" in the CPS adaptation of his song. It was sung to the tune of "John Brown's Body":

> When the Union's inspiration
> Through the campers' blood shall run,
> There can be no power greater
> Anywhere beneath the sun.
> Yet what force on earth is weaker
> Than the feeble strength of one?
> But the Union makes us strong.

Vincent S. Beck (center) with surveyors at Mancos Camp in 1944.

CHORUS
Solidarity forever!
Solidarity forever!
Solidarity forever!
For the Union makes us strong.

Is there aught we hold in common
With the tyrants we have here?
Who would crush us into serfdom
And would kick us in the rear?
We must organize a union
That these bums will learn to fear,
For the Union makes us strong.

Anti-Conscription

Seven of the songs specifically protest the draft and the Selective Service system. Probably "The Ballad of October 16" refers to the date in 1940 (actually it was September 16) when Congress passed the Selective Service Bill that resulted in the drafting of men for service in the armed forces of the United States. Both President Roosevelt and his wife Eleanor come in for criticism, as does J. P. Morgan. Since the notorious capitalist Morgan died in 1913, over thirty years before the Selective Service was formed, the emotional content of the song also incorporates the social discontent of the Great Depression. Perhaps stanza 3 even was sung by soldiers during World War I. The song is to be sung to the tune of "Jesse James's Death":

CHORUS:
It was on a Saturday night
And the moon was shining bright
When they passed that conscription bill,
And for miles and miles away,
Oh, you could hear the people say,
"'Twas the President and boys on
Capitol Hill."

Oh, Franklin Roosevelt
Told the people how he felt
And we damned near believed what he said.
He said, "I hate war and so does Eleanor,
But we won't be safe till everybody's dead."

When my dear old mother died,
I was sitting by her side,
And I promised her to war I'd never go.
Now I'm wearing khaki jeans
and eating army beans
And I'm told that J. P. Morgan loves me so.

Three of the anti-conscription songs single out Lewis B. Hershey, director of the Selective Service System, for specific criticism. "The Wickiup Artillery" is to be sung to the tune of "And the Caissons Go Rolling Along." The "dumpsters" were used in moving earth at the Lapine camp:

Over hill, over dale
We will hit the dusty trail
As those dumpsters go rolling along.
Laws are smashed, rules are bashed
And democracy is mashed
But the dumpsters go rolling along.

CHORUS
So it's work, work, work,
You poor old CO jerk,
Fighting for liberty.
Civilian Public Service
Makes everybody nervous
But the colonel from Washington, D.C.[4]

COs work all the day
But they don't get the pay,
Still the dumpsters go rolling along.

Hershey bars all around
Keep us guys from going to town.
Still the dumpsters go rolling along.

"Way Down upon the Deschutes River" refers to the stream
being dammed at Wickiup. Al Partridge, the composer, became
a professor at the University of Chicago after the war. The
words are to be sung to the tune of "Old Folks at Home."
"Reclamation" refers to the Bureau of Reclamation, under
which some CPS camps were administered:

Way down upon the Deschutes River
Far, far away.
That's where the COs do slave labor,
Working without pay.

CHORUS:
All the camp am sad and weary, . . .
Oh, Hershey, how our hearts grow weary,
Sponging on the old folks at home.

View from the air of buildings and grounds of Mancos Camp.

We're working for the Reclamation
Nine hours a day.
But we don't get no compensation.
Lord, we don't get no pay.

"Opposition to Conscription" is to be sung to the gospel tune "Down in My Heart":

I've got that opposition to conscription
Down in my heart, down in my heart,
Down in my heart.
I've got that opposition to conscription
Down in my heart,
Down in my heart to stay.

I know that Hershey doesn't like it but it's
Down in my heart, down in my heart,
Down in my heart.
I know that Hershey doesn't like it but it's
Down in my heart, down in my heart,
Down in my heart to stay.

Three other songs make more general complaints about conscription. "I Know Conscription's Wrong" simply adds a verse to "I'm Going Down the Road Feeling Bad":

I'm here, but I know conscription's wrong. (3 times)
Lord, Lord, I ain't gonna be treated this way.

I'm working for ten cents a day. (3 times)
Lord, Lord, I ain't gonna be treated this way.

They feed us on cornbread and beans. (3 times)
Lord, Lord, I ain't gonna be treated this way.

I'm going down that road feeling bad. (3 times)
Lord, Lord, I ain't gonna be treated this way.

"The CO Blues" by Dwight Rieman, is a similar lament, to be sung to the tune of "The St. Louis Blues":

> I've got those CO blues,
> I'm just as blue as blue can be.
> It's all because, it's all because, it's all because
> Of what Selective Service did to me.
> I signed old form 47
> Conscientiously, you see.
> Now see what Selective Service has done to me.
>
> They told me the work would be good.
> They sent me out to the woods
> And all I do is cut notches in trees,
> Cut notches until I'm down on my knees.
> And when it's 25 below
> Oh, Lord, how I do freeze.
>
> Now my gal she gave me the air.
> I can no longer look on her face so fair.
> She tossed me aside like a battered toy
> And gave her heart to a soldier boy.
>
> I'm getting bluer day by day
> And I don't know how long it will be
> Before I get out of this mess.
> But the man who signs my release
> The Lord will surely bless.

"Kill, Kill, Kill," by Frank Hatfield, is to be sung to the tune of "Old Black Joe." Although the concluding line no doubt refers to war-mongers, it is ambiguous enough to also express the angry frustration of campers who feel that they are giving "involuntary servitude":

> Gone are the days when I had my liberty.
> I am a slave in the country of the free.

Gone are the truths that now I cling to still.
I hear once-gentle voices shouting, "Kill! Kill! Kill!"

CHORUS:
Conscription, conscription,
It takes away man's will
And bows his soul to voices shouting,
"Kill! Kill! Kill!"

Camp Topical Songs

Four of the songs deal with the specifics of life at Camp Wickiup. "Old Man Olsen Had a Camp," to be sung to the tune of "Old McDonald," refers to the Mennonite "good boys," and is the song Vincent and his friends heard sung at their first meal at Camp Wickiup. Col. Olsen was director of the camp during its transition from Mennonite to government administration.

Old Man Olsen had a camp,
E-I-E-I-O.
And in this camp were Mennonites,
E-I-E-I-O.
With yes, yes, here, a yes, yes, there.
here a yes, there a yes, everywhere a yes, yes.
Old Man Olsen had a camp,
E-I-E-I-O.

Old Man Olsen had a camp,
E-I-E-I-O.
And in this camp there was a bell,
E-I-E-I-O.
With a ding, ding, here, a dong, dong there,
here a ding, there a dong, everywhere a ding, dong.
Old Man Olsen had a camp, E-I-E-I-O.

Old Man Olsen had a camp,
E-I-E-I-O.
And in this camp there were Mancosites,

E-I-E-I-O.
With a no, no, here, a no, no, there,
here a no, there a no, everywhere a "Hell no!"
Old Man Olsen had a camp,
E-I-E-I-O.

In "I've Been Working in the Timber," to be sung to the tune of "I've Been Working on the Railroad," Col. Olsen asks a heavyset camper named Tiny to announce mealtime by blowing his trumpet:

I've been working in the timber
All the livelongday.
I've been working in the timber
but I can't get any pay.
Can't you hear those bells a-ringing
So early in the morn?
Can't you hear Old Man Olsen shouting,
"Tiny. Blow your horn"?

Olsen was eventually replaced by Herbert Murch as director of Camp Wickiup.

The speaker in the song "4F and SQ" by Frank Hatfield is

Buildings and grounds at Camp Wickiup, CPS #128, Lapine, Oregon.

a sick camper whose illness is thought by camp officials to be mere avoidance of work. "4F" refers to draftees who are physically unfit. "SQ" refers to sick quarters. "RTW" is an abbreviation for "refuse to work." After three RTWs a camper went to prison. Gilmore was the camp cook. The words are to be sung to the tune of "Pistol Packin' Mamma":

> The doctor pulled my teeth all out,
> he found me heart was bad.
> He looked at me and said, "T.B."
> and even thought me mad.
>
> CHORUS;
> Oh, get those 4Fs through, Murch,
> get those 4F's through.
> For I've been here a half a year
> and always been SQ.
>
> Eating starch in the dining hall
> and I am bound up tight.
> I am so weak my bones do creak
> yet Gilmore wants to fight.
>
> "Now boys, don't get impatient,"
> our layman doctor said.
> But I'm so weak my bones do creak,
> and I can't get out of bed.
>
> Now, boys, while you are waiting
> you cannot go SQ.
> So do light work or else, you jerk,
> It's R – T – W.
>
> Now rigor mortis has set in,
> my bones are stiff and cold.
> I have gangrene, as all have seen,
> yet I'm not sick, I'm told.

And that's the way it goes, boys,
that's just what he said.
So rest in peace, for your release
will come when you are dead.

LAST CHORUS:
Oh, get those coffins made, Murch,
get those coffins made,
For I'm not strong, I've not got long
before I will be dead.

"Johnny Boy," to be sung to the tune of "Billy Boy," refers to John Calef, a six-foot, blond Wickiup camper who was caught sunbathing in the nude between the dormitory buildings one weekend. Even though there were no women at the camp, a camp official turned him over to the Bend, Oregon, police, who jailed him for a short time.

Oh, where have you gone, Johnny boy, Johnny boy?
O, where here you gone, Johnny Calef?
Some filthy-minded prude
Said he saw you in the nude.
You're a young thing and shouldn't leave your mother.

Do you want to go to jail, Johnny boy, Johnny boy?
Do you want to go to jail, Johnny Calef?
Except for SQ
It will seem the same to you.
You have gone from one prison to another.

Are you sorry to be gone, Johnny boy, Johnny boy?
Are you sorry to be gone, Johnny Calef?
You really shouldn't care.
The administration won't be there.
That is something that should make you happy, Brother.

Three Consequences of Protest

Three songs consider the consequences of noncooperation with camp authorities. "Who's Going Next?" considers the option of being put in a local jail, as Johnny Calef had been. Uncle Elmer in stanza 2 was a government crew leader—a "nice little old man," according to Vincent. Pollard in stanza 3 was a government bookkeeper. Herbert Murch, the Wickiup camp director, is accused here of relishing the notion of COs being hanged, although Vincent concedes that he was a decent man just "doing his duty":

> 'Twas at a camp named Wickiup
> And all the lads were there
> Raising holy blazes
> In the middle of Murch's hair.
>
> CHORUS:
> Singing, "Who's going next, lads?
> Who's going to jail?
> You'd better be a-ready
> With your pockets full of bail."
>
> And Uncle Elmer came along
> A-driving through the fog
> And who should be a-sittin' there
> Behind him but his dog.
>
> And Pollard was a-sittin' there
> A-messin' up the books
> And when he couldn't balance 'em
> He blamed it on the cooks.
>
> And Herby Murch was also there and
> Very pleased to see
> Four-and-twenty COs
> A-hangin' from a tree.

Two songs concern the ultimate consequences of noncooperation—being transferred to the camp at Germfask, Michigan, designed to hold the worst of the "bad boys." "M-I-C-H-I-G-A-N," composed by Frank Hatfield, was to be sung to the Notre Dame fight song:

> M-I-C-H-I-G-A-N.
> We all know that this will be the end—
> One-way passage to Germfask,
> The cold-storage spot for the bad-boy class.
>
> We don't believe that slavery is right.
> We fight it in our own way, with might.
> So off to Michigan are we
> And onward to liberty.

"Our Old and Dusty Loam," to be sung to the tune of "My Old Kentucky Home," vows to continue the program of noncooperation begun by the bad-boy "slobs" and "brains" that had been transferred to the Germfask camp:

> Oh, the bad boys are gone
> from the forests of Lapine.
> They've left for a camp in Michigan.
> The director thinks
> all the brains have gone with them,
> But we'll carry on the work the "slobs" began.
>
> CHORUS
> So, weep no more for Mancos.
> The brains are not all gone.
> We will sing this song to our friends so far away
> and the fight which they began.
> Carry on!

Vincent liked these songs because they were "pretty cleverly written" and "made a point in a humorous way." Until 2003, when he was disabled by a stroke and eventually died, he still sang some of them without looking at the printed texts. In the summer of 1995 he performed "4F and SQ" at a talent night program at the Mennonite camp Little Eden near Onekama, Michigan, where he had a summer home.

Vincent lamented what he sensed to be a diminished peace emphasis in the Mennonite Church. He sustained his own peace convictions by supporting the National Interreligious Service Board for Conscientious Objectors and subscribing to the newsletter *The Reporter for Conscience' Sake*. He was articulate in discussing developments in national and international conscientious objection. The songs became an emotional expression of this interest, a direct tie with his earlier life experience, and one means by which Vincent moved from being a "nonresistant" to a "nonviolent" objector to war.

Protest Songs as Mennonite Folklore

The songs in Vincent's collection conform to what is generally known about traditional songs of protest. They emerge from occupational groups, in this case manual laborers in

Men at Camp Wickiup. Vincent S. Beck is fifth from left in the back row.

enforced circumstances. They are often composed by known authors, five of whom are remembered in the collection, with Frank Hatfield being given credit for three of the songs. They exploit previously known tunes, here including folksongs ("Old Macdonald Had a Farm"), hymns ("Onward, Christian Soldiers"), and popular songs ("Pistol Packin' Mama"). Most important for folklore, they were embraced by a community of people as effective expressive forms and were transmitted informally, both "by ear" and by manuscript.[5]

These protest songs are a bit unusual, however, because, although they do object to hard work for no pay, their main concern is the political system that has brought the workers and singers to "involuntary servitude." They are really political protest songs, objecting not only to the politics of warfare but also to the capitalist and religious systems that lie behind the war. They carry with them a veiled agenda associated with the early U.S. labor movement as well as the Marxist/socialist politics that emerged between the two world wars.

With the end of the war and conscription, the occupational group ceased to exist and the songs lost their usefulness.

Work crew at Mancos Camp. Vincent S. Beck is at far right.

Vincent's typewritten manuscript may be the only form in which the CPS protest songs have survived that particular situation of use. But as with many other protest songs, perhaps they became transmuted once more, adapted to the needs of the popular movements for civil rights and against the Vietnam War. For instance, "Solidarity Forever" has been an especially adaptable song, surviving into the present and having been used in many different contexts, since its origin in 1915.[6]

What is the significance of Vincent's custodianship of the songs for Mennonites and Mennonite folklore?

Vincent deserves credit for being what folklorists call a "strong tradition bearer." That is. he was a person who, more so than most of his compatriots, was aware of the value of orally transmitted materials and committed himself to save and use them despite his own community's passive neglect of them. Vincent remembered and sang them whenever he could. And he was most grateful when this essay was first published in *Mennonite Life*. He felt vindicated, both for his resistant attitude toward some aspects of CPS and for saving the manuscript of songs through fifty-eight years.

His songs certainly are not "Mennonite folklore" in the conventional sense, since the Mennonite community at large has never heard of them, let alone used them. Even the overwhelming majority of Mennonite men and women who served in CPS are unaware of the songs. In the context of the Mennonite community, his songs actually are expressive forms that contradict communal values. The average Mennonite would wince upon hearing the harsh images in "Christians at War" or rough language like "that pack of G...D fools." Historically, Mennonites opposed the labor movement and Marxism, because of their threat to use violence to attain their end, and would certainly not endorse songs that support such politics.

Although, as noted earlier, the songs had personal values of self-vindication for Vincent, they also preserved for posterity a vivid sense of life in some CPS camps. And their sentiments increasingly complement the more active peacemaking efforts developed in recent years by Mennonite church institutions, especially the Christian Peacemaker Teams and the peace studies programs at Mennonite colleges. "Peace and Justice," not "nonresistance," is the new Mennonite motto—the former echoing the "bad boys" and the latter echoing the "good boys" of CPS.

With their publication, the songs' usefulness may move beyond Vincent's personal therapy and become agents for further change within the Mennonite church. The published songs have drawn the attention of professors of peace studies at some colleges, which pleased Vincent.

The songs will likely not become standard elements in the Mennonite folksong repertoire, but they might be respectfully claimed by Mennonites today. In particular, those who conduct the Mennofolk Music Festival, mentioned in the introduction to this book, might want to revive them in public performance for a new group of Mennonite folk.

·7·

Painting on Glass

The Old Order Amish are the most iconoclastic heirs of the Zwinglian Reformation. The Swiss Brethren (Mennonites), who separated from Ulrich Zwingli in 1525, continued his ban on images in religious worship. The Amish, who separated from the Mennonites in 1693-97, have gone even further in rejecting pictorial art.

Their literal interpretation of the Second Commandment, forbidding "graven images," has led them to forgo the use of photography and to refuse to have themselves—and sometimes also their possessions—photographed by others. Historically, in their folk arts they refrain from depicting the human form and they represent objects from nature in a highly stylized, rather than realistic, manner. The best examples, of course, are antique Amish quilts, which are almost always of geometrical design.

Given such an image-denying culture, it is somewhat surprising that many Amish communities have supported a tradition of pictorial folk art painted on glass in the form of mottos and commemorative records. True, the pictorial elements are usually flowers, birds, and butterflies that decorate moral statements, rather than full-blown landscapes or other pictures presented as art for art's sake. But in light of the scarcity of pictorial wall art in folk cultures in general, and given the traditional Amish suspicion of images, their painted glass offers an opportunity to study the role of folk art and folk artists in a culture that is suspicious of art for moral and religious reasons.

The photographs accompanying this essay illustrate three different glass painting techniques. Most paintings shown here are often called "tinsel" or "foil" paintings. As shown in figures 1, 2, and others, they are actually reverse paintings on glass with a tinfoil backing. First the artist outlines the design with india ink or black oil paint on the back side of the glass, and paints the background area with opaque paint. Then she paints some areas with colored opaque paints, other areas with translucent colored paint, and leaves some areas unpainted. Prior to about 1945, most backgrounds were black (fig. 10); recently, almost all have been white.

Before the painting is framed, a sheet of crinkled foil is inserted between the painting and the cardboard backing. In earlier years, the foil came from discarded cigarette and gum wrappers; recently it has come from rolls of aluminum foil. The foil backing shines silver through the unpainted areas and shiny-colored through the areas painted with translucent paint.

Since all paint is applied to the back side of the glass, the basic technique is known as reverse glass painting in English, *Hinterglasmalerai* (behind-glass-writing) in standard German, and *hinrich schreiva* (backward writing) or *hinna seit schreiva* (back side writing) in the Pennsylvania German dialect spoken as a native language by Amish glass painters. However, the term most commonly used by Amish for these paintings is *mottos*.

A second, more currently popular technique is illustrated by figures 8 and 9. In these, text and pictorial elements are applied to the top side of the glass with tubes of liquid embroidery paint. An opaque background—sometimes white, often pastel—is sprayed onto the back side of the glass, sometimes with mar-belized or shaded effects. The painting is then framed with ladder chain, whose squarish links firmly grip all four edges of the glass.

A third technique, used by only a few artists, incorporates elements from the other two in a kind of composite medium. As in figure 7, text and decorations are applied to the back side of the glass. No translucent paints are used. And in place of a sheet of tinfoil, the silvery effect is achieved by gluing bits of silver glitter on to certain areas. That makes it possible for the painting to be framed with ladder chain rather than with a conventional frame.

All three techniques result in paintings with glossy, sparkling surfaces. Because it is difficult to attain depth of field in glass painting, painted areas appear "flat," although in tinsel painting the crinkled foil backing adds some feeling of depth to the design.

Glass painting is an ancient art that originated, apparently, with the invention of glass making in ancient Syria. Its religious use in the west began with Christian portrait medallions such as those found in the catacombs of Rome, continued with glass-painted icons in Byzantium, and flourished as a fine art in the European Renaissance and Reformation. By 1700, painting on glass for devotional purposes became a popular art produced in glassmaking centers in Germany, Slovakia, Austria, and elsewhere.

Catholic and Protestant uses differed significantly, however. Catholic paintings on glass depicted the human form, whether in portraits of the saints or in scenes from the Bible. They were typically displayed in the *Hergottswinkel* (God's corner) of the house, a devotional area decorated with holy pictures and ceramic plates.

Protestant glass paintings in Europe normally eschewed the human form and most pictorial representation, presenting instead scriptural, moral, or historical writings in fine calligraphy, with occasional linear flourishes or floral decorations. European Protestants, especially Lutherans, typically hung these paintings in the "Bible corner" of a house, along with a portrait of Luther and other inducements to devotion. The Amish and Mennonite glass paintings presented here clearly fit within this tradition of design and function.

However, they are apparently not part of an unbroken continuity with these European paintings. Although some of the earliest Anabaptists were professional painters on glass, and although both the Amish and Mennonites came from Switzerland and Alsace, where glass painting flourished, no evidence suggests that they brought this folk art with them from Europe and continued its manufacture in the United States. Instead, glass painting apparently emerged among them in America only since about 1930 as the result of various influences from popular, folk, and fine art of the early twentieth century.

First, of course, were other glass painting traditions in American culture. Chief among them were the Catholic and Protestant glass paintings made and used by other religious groups, particularly in German-speaking cultures. Amish and Mennonites must have seen—and occasionally even used—these paintings in their homes. Various glass-painting traditions were also present in English-speaking American culture. They include scenes painted on the glass of clock cases, lithographs converted to glass paintings in the China trade, romantic European landscapes apparently imported from Europe, and floral still lifes probably made at home by women during the nineteenth century.

The most important influence may have been instruction in the craft given to Amish and Mennonite students in elementary schools. The December 1930 issue of *The School Arts Magazine,* for instance, describes "How to Make Pictures of Glorified Glass." The instructions yield a black silhouette scene backed with tinfoil and cardboard and framed with bookbinding (passepartout) tape.

One Mennonite teacher recalls being taught how to do foil painting in an elementary education course at Western Oregon University 1934. She found it an attractive kind of project because it used readily available, inexpensive materials and kept her students busy over several days' time while the various colors of paint dried. I know of Mennonite teachers who taught this craft to Mennonite and Amish students in the 1930s in places as far-flung as Oregon, Indiana, and Maryland.

The way school craft became homegrown folk art is suggested by one Mennonite informant from Iowa who learned glass painting in public elementary school, taught her mother at home, and then watched her mother and aunt develop glass-painted mottos in a kind of friendly rivalry. The main difference between school and home art is that the school tradition was apparently entirely pictorial, whereas the home tradition almost invariably featured a motto or Scripture text, with pictorial elements for decoration. Here we see again how folk artists borrow a technique from one context and then deliberately adapt it according to the tastes, needs, and values of another.

As a school and home art, the technique was also supported by manufacturers of foil paintings and by craft supply houses, both of which served a nationwide market. As late as 1958, the catalog for Thayer and Chandler of Chicago urged readers to "Paint Glorified Glass Pictures for Profit. Popular—Easy to Do—Astonishing Results." It offered patterns for silhouettes and conventional scenes (but no mottos) as well as supplies such as pieces of glass, oriental lacquers, glass emulsion for outlining, passepartout tape, and picture frames. Apparently Thayer and Chandler was the major source of supplies for Amish and Mennonite painters on glass. When it discontinued the sale of oriental lacquers about thirty years ago, many glass painters stopped working.

Finally, twentieth-century glass painting in both popular art and folk art may have been inspired by developments in western fine art at the same time and a bit earlier. In the early 1900s, for instance, Wassily Kandinsky, and Paul Klee, among others, revived reverse glass painting after being attracted by the bright, flat colors of European folk paintings on glass. A more influential revival occurred in the 1920s in France, during the Art Deco movement, when painters such as Rene Buthaud and Jean Dupas revived interest in the technique. Dupas' history of navigation, painted on glass for the salon of the ocean liner *Normandie* and now partly preserved in the restaurant area of the Metropolitan Museum of Art, is one monument to the revival of reverse painting on glass. It helps us see that both popular and folk uses of the medium were part of a widespread appreciation during the Art Deco period of flat, hard, glossy, decorative surfaces.

That may not be what one would normally expect from people otherwise committed to a "plain" aesthetic, but the fact remains that the painting of mottos and commemorative records in this glittering, showy medium was very popular among Mennonites and Amish from about 1930 to 1960. It continues today as a barely surviving tradition among Amish folk artists in some communities in northern Indiana, from which come all of the illustrations shown here, as well as isolated communities in Pennsylvania and Michigan.

The designs of these paintings represent "copyist" art, since they are not drawn freehand but derive from preexisting patterns—as do many other folk arts, of course, including the fraktur tradition in Pennsylvania German culture. Sometimes the copying of a pattern is strict, as when glass painters simply trace the design off a lithographed moral wall decoration. Usually, however, the process is more creative. Sometimes glass artists take a large single design from Thayer and Chandler and add a suitable text. Most boxes of glass-painting patterns that I have seen contain separate decorative elements (flowers, birds, flourishes) that can be combined in creative ways with various texts to form new paintings. Often, then, the patterns for these paintings are transmitted whole from artist to artist, although each new rendering is made unique by alterations in coloring, adjustments in the design to fit the size of the frame being used, and minor rearrangements of text or decoration.

Some overall tendencies emerge in the hundreds of glass paintings that I have seen. First, pictorial elements are as prominent as verbal ones in Amish work. This contrasts with the earlier word-dominated Protestant paintings and is striking when one considers the general Amish suspicion of imagery. Second, the pictorial elements are almost always images from nature, especially birds, flowers, plants, and butterflies—nature in its smiling aspect. Full landscapes are rare, especially in Amish work, but more common in Mennonite work. The human fig-

ure is almost universally absent in Amish painting but sometimes present in Mennonite painting. And overt symbolism is
generally lacking in Amish designs, although often present in
Mennonite designs.

Even though the pictorial elements are impressive, this is
essentially an art form dedicated to transforming verbal truth
into beauty. In fact, the verbal element is so powerful that even
in those rare instances where glass paintings lack words (fig. 1),
Amish artists invariably call them "mottos." Fine—usually
fancy—lettering, therefore, is a criterion of achievement in such
work, whether it follows Gothic, Spencerian, Hallmark, or
newspaper banner styles.

Most of the texts are Scripture passages, with the Lord's
Prayer probably the most common. Following in popularity are
moral and religious sayings, such as "Jesus Saves" or "Trust and
Obey." In addition, glass paintings often display house blessings, praise of motherhood, statements of friendship and, occasionally, popular secular verse.

A different category of glass paintings records family history.
Marriage records, birth records, family genealogies, death
memorials, and wedding anniversary records are common, as
are birthday and Father's and Mother's Day greetings. Such
records are made only by Amish, not by Mennonite, glass
artists, probably because they take the place of photographs in
creating a permanent record of transitional rites for these
photograph-renouncing people.

In a fully documented article in *The Mennonite Quarterly
Review*, I discuss in greater detail much of the above and also
speculate on what glass painting communicates about the
changing aesthetics, culture, sociology, and theology of Amish
and Mennonites.[1] In this chapter I focus on the lives and work
of five living glass artists in order to show how, by whom, and
to what effect such folk art is produced in these "plain" communities. Although this survey of artists focuses on the dynamic,
contemporary human element of the tradition, it also implies a
great deal in regard to the larger topics mentioned above.

The tinsel paintings of **Mary Yoder Miller** (b. 1931) are among the most interesting from the Amish community because of their careful execution, creative design, and large size (her peacock, fig. 1, is 20 in. x 23 in.). Mary learned glass painting when she was seventeen years old from Mary Christner (1897-1979), a Mennonite who managed the Honeyville General Store.

Following her marriage, she also began making commemorative family records in the medium. Between 1948 and 1975, when she quit because of weakened eyesight, she made 219 paintings for Amish friends and relatives throughout the midwest at prices ranging from one to fifteen dollars.

Mary's work was highly collaborative. At first, she worked with her sister-in-law Katie Miller Schlabach (b. 1932), with whom she developed and traded patterns. Both Mary and Katie used the help of Katie's mother Anna J., who was known for her fine handwriting. In making family records, they usually asked Anna to do the handwriting for them. In exchange, they did baking for her or helped with housecleaning. Later, Mary enlisted the help of her husband and children in designing patterns, doing careful handwriting and helping with repetitious painting.

In addition to teaching others the craft, Mary has been a conservator of the art in other ways. For instance, she chose to continue to do reverse painting when painting on top of glass became more popular in her community. Also, she remained actively interested in her daughter's tinsel painting and exerted a conservative influence over her. When her daughter was thinking of using a new design for a birth announcement, Mary said something like, "Oh, I'd use this one instead," and her daughter used the old design.

Figure 1. PEACOCK. This striking painting of a peacock is unusual in many ways. Mary Miller got the pattern for it from her teacher Mary Christner, who kept peacocks in the yard of the Honeyville Store. Although the pattern may originally have come from an embroidered dresser scarf, it is related to images from much earlier Pennsylvania German folk art, in which the peacock was a traditional image in fraktur work, and the design of classical columns supporting an arch was found on many decorated blanket chests. It is also one of the few Amish glass paintings without a motto. Why? "You know, I've always wondered myself," Mary says. Despite the painting's lack of words, Mary still calls it a "motto."

Mary is unaware of the ancient association of the peacock with the phoenix and, in turn, of the phoenix with the resurrected Christ. The peacock apparently has a less noble meaning in Amish culture. As Mary's husband recalls, "We had a preacher when I was a kid. He was from Kansas and he said, 'Now, just like a peacock. He goes and struts, you know. And you'd tell him he isn't as pretty as he thinks he is. Just look at your dirty feet.'" Amish preachers sometimes refer in their sermons to mottos hanging on the walls of the house in which a Sunday worship service is being held. Since Mary's peacock hung in a bedroom rather than the living room, it may have escaped being used as an object lesson in humility.

Figure 2. HOLY MATRIMONY. Mary Miller's marriage record design came from her sister-in-law, who adapted it from a late-nineteenth-century printed wedding record. Mary's son created the open book shapes to replace the ovals from the lithograph. Mary added the bow to the design. Mary's mother-in-law added "Peace be unto you," borne by the bird, and also created the lettering with the squiggles below and above the text "to make it look a little fancier."

The Amish marriage record retains all the text of the original but adds a section for table-waiters at the bottom. In Amish weddings friends of the bride and groom are asked to wait on tables during the wedding reception and are regarded as official members of the wedding party. Such wedding records are often gifts from parents to the newlyweds and are first publicly displayed behind the *Eck*, or corner table, where the wedding party sits during the wedding reception.

Figures 3 and 4. "OUR FATHER." This is the favorite motto of Mary's family. "I doubt it if money can buy that," says her husband. It was a wedding gift to them from his sister Katie, who adapted the design from the nineteenth-century lithograph of the Lord's Prayer shown here. Katie's pattern preserves the print's layout of the text but adds entirely different decorations. In place of the Ten Commandments (with human subjects) that surround the lithographed text, the Amish artists have added a bow and images from nature—birds, flowers, foliage, and butterflies. This is the most widespread foil-painting design in northern Indiana.

Katie Schmucker Miller (b. 1956) began tinsel painting in April 1986 because she wanted to earn some extra money. The mother of five children, fourteen years old and younger, Katie lives in the small village of Emma in LaGrange County. She learned the rudiments of foil painting by spending a day with her teacher at her aunt's house, then having the teacher come to her own house for a day.

Although her teacher had inherited all of Mary Miller's patterns, Katie borrowed only a few from her. She made most of her own patterns. She found most of the design elements in her mother's collection of quilt block and embroidery patterns. She also used pictures from coloring books published for Amish children. Yet despite the innovative nature of her work, it remains very traditional in its use of texts and designs.

Like Mary Miller, Katie also relied heavily on collaboration with family and friends. Friends helped her by finding inexpensive frames for her at garage sales. Her brother sometimes made frames, and her sister did all of the lettering. In fact, once a week Katie met with her sister at her mother's house in order to give her sister the orders for the next week and collect the letter designs that she requested of her the previous week.

Katie marketed her work in many ways. She used some paintings as birthday and friendship gifts. Family and friends ordered mottos directly from her. She sold some at other people's garage sales. She placed others at Amish country stores operated by her friends or relatives. The farthest she went in marketing her paintings beyond the Amish community was the Galarina Arts store in Shipshewana, which caters to tourists. But even there they were sold mainly to Amish customers, which indicates that, despite the current American craze for "folk art," the taste for glass painting mottos has not moved beyond the Amish community. In her first four months of glass painting, Katie sold fifty mottos.

Figure 5. TEN COMMANDMENTS. "The Ten Commandments" is one of the most popular and elaborate of Katie Miller's mottos. She copied the script from a print version but added flowers of her own choosing, apparently from an embroidery design. Katie uses deeply crinkled foil behind her paintings, which gives them a more three-dimensional effect than is found in the work of other artists.

Sarah Ellen Troyer (b. 1940) is an unmarried Amish woman who supports herself by making patterns for new cloth products in the mobile home industry. From 1962 until 1983 Sarah Ellen made glass mottos for her Amish community. She apparently originated the composite glass-painting technique described above.

Sarah Ellen learned painting on top of glass from her Conservative Mennonite neighbor Mary Bontrager, who once gave her a small motto, "What a Friend We Have in Jesus," for helping her with spring housecleaning. Sarah Ellen soon became a major supplier of mottos for her community. She made over 500 such mottos, sometimes as many as 100 per year. At the peak of her production, she was ordering $100 worth of ladder chain at a time. In fact, orders were so heavy that what started out to be a hobby for her eventually became a chore. "I always felt obligated to do it," Sarah Ellen says. When she felt that she absolutely must quit painting on glass, she found that she could not merely say no and stop. Instead, she says, "I made sure I was out of chain and I started saying no."

Figure 6. THIS IS THE DAY. No regulations forbid Amish use of new household crafts as they become popular in mainstream American culture. They now make mottos and family records in wood-burning, velvet painting, shadow box, and other faddish media. Here Sarah Ellen Troyer adapted the motto tradition to painting on wood decorated with a dried bouquet.

Figure 7. SISTER SUSIE BONTRAGER. This death record blends the techniques of foil painting and painting on top of glass. The verses come from the obituary section of *The Budget*, the weekly newspaper published in Sugarcreek, Ohio, that serves the international Amish community. Although the design comes from Mary Miller's pattern box, it ultimately derives from memorial cards prepared by an Amish printer in Pennsylvania for Amish customers throughout the United States.

Waneta Miller (b. 1968) has had a typical glass-painting career for an Amish woman. In 1982, she completed eight grades of education, four in public school and four in her district's Amish school. When she stopped going to school, she took up glass painting, both as a diversion and as a means of earning money. Actually, she was asked to learn the craft by Sarah Ellen Troyer, and Waneta eagerly accepted the offer. Sarah Ellen and Waneta are neighbors and Waneta's parents used to sell Sarah Ellen's mottos in Miller's Country Store, which they operated first in a separate, garage-like building behind their house and now in a large building in an adjacent lot.

The demand for Waneta's mottos was greater than she could supply. She gave away many for Christmas, birthday, and wedding gifts. She frequently received orders for multiple copies of the same item—as from a Conservative Mennonite Bible School teacher for all of her students and from parents who ordered the same motto as a gift for all of their children. At Christmas time she was unable to fill all the orders she received. Waneta's parents were forced by demand to augment their stock by purchasing glass mottos by mail from a woman in Pennsylvania.

Inside the Town Line Fabric Store, located between Goshen and Emma, Indiana, Katie Miller's mottos hang above a display of notions.

Mary Miller's dining area contains six glass-door cupboards full of colorful plates and glassware, mostly antique. Six of Mary's glittering tinsel paintings fit in harmoniously with this glass-dominated décor. Here "The Lord's Prayer" dominates the sideboard and dining area of the room, offering a fitting devotional focus for mealtime. The kind and number of items permitted on the walls of houses depends upon the rules of each Amish district. Mary's district allows some mottos on the walls but not "great big paintings" or "scenery bought in the store."

Figure 2. Holy Matrimony.

Figure 1. Peacock.

Figure 3. Oval "Our Father."

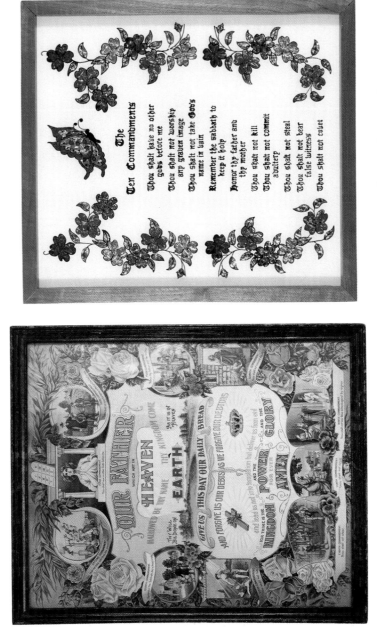

Figure 5. The Ten Commandments.

Figure 4. Square litho "Our Father."

Figure 7. Sister Susie Bontrager.

Figure 6. This Is the Day.

Danket dem Herrn
denn Er ist
freundlich, und Seine
Güte währet ewiglich.

Ps. 107:1

Figure 8. Danket dem Herrn.

FAMILY RECORD

HOWARD MILLER   and   LILLIAN NISLEY
May 1, 1942   April 3, 1940

WERE UNITED IN MARRIAGE — DECEMBER 20, 1962

TO THIS UNION WERE BORN

KATHRYN - OCTOBER 6, 1963   NORMAN - MAY 7, 1974
                                   died - NOVEMBER 14, 1975
LAVERA - NOVEMBER 30, 1964
                                   NELSON - MAY 7, 1974
KENNETH - stillborn - MAY 20, 1966 died - DECEMBER 7, 1975

WANETA - APRIL 7, 1968   MIRIAM - stillborn - OCTOBER 10, 1976

ORVAN - JANUARY 2, 1970   PERRY LEE - JUNE 2, 1978

ESTHER - stillborn - NOVEMBER 26, 1971   EDITH - JULY 22, 1980

Figure 9. Family Record.

Town Line Fabric Store.

Lloyd and Norma Jean Ressler in front of a Conservative Mennonite
Church near Nappanee, Indiana.

Figure 10. Love One Another As I Have Loved You.

Figure 11. Let the Lord be Magnified.

After making about 300 mottos in three years, in 1986 Waneta stopped making them in large quantities and now makes them only for special occasions. She quit because the demand was so high and because she made too little profit to justify continuing the work as a leisure-time activity. She was relieved when her cousins became interested in learning the art and taking over her business. Waneta is now married and has stopped doing painting on glass.

When I asked Waneta if she ever signed her name on a motto, she replied, "People don't have to know who made it." To which her mother added, "Artists do. But actually this is just copying a pattern." They could think of no word in their Pennsylvania German dialect for "art," and had to resort to a dictionary to find the standard German equivalent, *Kunst*. To them, art means freehand drawing—"the kind found in museums."

Figure 8. DANKET DEM HERRN. The translation of this motto painted on top of glass is, "O thank the Lord, for he is good, and his mercy endures forever." It is the favorite motto of Waneta's customers. The verse is used in almost every worship service in her Amish district. Glass mottos written in German are unusual, since the Amish speak a German dialect that has no conventional written form and are often unable to read much standard German.

Figure 9. FAMILY RECORD. The scroll design is a typical one for Amish genealogies painted on top of glass. It took Waneta Miller a full day to make a family record like this. Although it looks like the technique of painting on top of glass, on this record all of the design is painted on the back side instead.

Loyal Ressler (b. 1929) of rural Nappanee, Indiana, is a Conservative Mennonite farmer and tinsel painter. He did most of his painting on glass between 1953 and 1956, when he was working in the kitchen of the Irene Byron Hospital in Fort Wayne. As a conscientious objector (CO) to military service, he had gone there to fulfill his government requirement of alternative civilian service—called I-W work, after the Selective Service category assigned to men granted CO status by their draft boards. While living in close fellowship with the many kinds of Mennonites and Amish who were there doing the same kind of work, Loyal learned glass painting and produced hundreds of mottos for the I-W men and their families who came to visit them.

"I sold and sold to I-W's and Mennonite people," he says. "People would think it foolish to have pictures on the wall. Pictures wouldn't have gone over at all. That's why these mottos took very well." Loyal's mottos are a logical extension of his commitment to evangelical Christianity. "When I became a Christian, I went into spiritual things—that would have a meaning for people."

Loyal even made some mottos for Mennonite meetinghouses in the Fort Wayne area. Bearing verses such as "Let the Lord Be Magnified" and "This Is the House of the Lord," these mottos were hung on the front wall of the sanctuaries—near the attendance boards that used to dominate every Mennonite pulpit area—as inducements to worship.

Following the interest I showed in his work, Loyal once again brought out his homemade light box and patterns and found craft paints to substitute for the oriental lacquers that he once used. But he still has a large box full of unused, unsold mottos that he made long ago. And it is unlikely that his paintings will find ready acceptance today among his fellow Conservative Mennonites, who are now more interested in paintings on velvet and, indeed, in the "foolish pictures" that they earlier condemned.

Figure 10. LOVE ONE ANOTHER. This is a very typical design for a tinsel painting motto. The black background is typical of Protestant mottos made by reverse glass painting since the early Reformation. It was also typical for Indiana and Amish glass paintings until about 1945. Since then, white backgrounds have become the norm.

Figure 11. LET THE LORD BE MAGNIFIED. Loyal Ressler made this motto for the Anderson Mennonite Church near Fort Wayne, which he attended and where it hung for many years. The meetinghouse drawn in the insert is based on a picture of the First Mennonite Church of Fort Wayne printed on its Sunday bulletin.

Indiana Amish Family Records

Since the Old Order Amish reject formal education (normally not attending school beyond the eighth grade), they have produced virtually no written histories of themselves or other people. Most histories of the Amish have been written by Mennonites.

In writing genealogies and family histories, however, the Amish are extremely active and interested. David Luthy, Amish editor and librarian from Aylmer, Ontario, observes that "most Amish homes have at least one family record book (genealogy) among the books on their shelves." Luthy has identified at least 368 Amish family histories published between 1885-1977, many of them written by Amish. They continue to appear at the rate of about ten per year.[1] Genealogy is "their most vigorous form of history," said the late John Oyer, Mennonite historian and editor of the *Mennonite Quarterly Review*.

An even more impressive Amish achievement in genealogy, however, lies in the family histories memorized by Amish people and transmitted orally by them from generation to generation. Some older Amish people are amazing storehouses of information about intricate family relationships, and their conversations frequently dwell upon who is related to whom, and through what ancestors.

The records of Amish family history depicted on the following pages—birth, wedding, family, and memorial records—are counterparts in folk art of the folk histories of Amish families that the Amish community relishes. Since they present little more than vital statistics, their contribution to formal, academic history-writing is modest. But for the Amish homes in which they are hung they embody greater significance, as some aspects of Amish sociology and culture will clarify.

First, they nurture family identity and cohesiveness, which is a primary value among the Amish since it is through family structure that Amish beliefs and values are most intimately and effectively perpetuated.

Most Amish, of course, are "born" into the Amish faith; few are converts from the "English" world. That creates a religious community that is relatively homogeneous and stable in ethnic stock. Indeed, John A. Hostetler, Mennonite sociologist, pointed out that among the 144,000 Amish in America in the early 1990s there appeared only 126 different family names, and 18 of those names were represented by only one household.[2]

Amish settlement patterns are family-related in special ways. Three generations often live in an Amish household. Amish church districts are organized according to number of families, not individuals. And since families tend to settle in their blood relatives' communities, and since horse-and-buggy transportation encourages density in Amish settlements, family connections remain strong even after offspring marry and leave their parents' households. For instance, in each of the three largest Amish communities in the United States—eastern Ohio, Lancaster County, Pennsylvania, and north-central Indiana—over half of the population represent only five different family names.[3]

Artistically, the records embody additional importance. Since most of the records pictured here were made within the past three generations, they testify to the active, valued presence of folk artists in the Amish community. Most of these records were made for pay by Amish folk artists, which is interesting in light of the otherwise low status traditionally assigned to art by the Amish.

Although the earliest record shown here dates from about 1867, and although Lancaster County Amish used wall-hung family records in the nineteenth century, the making and displaying of family history records is a relatively new development among Indiana Old Order Amish. Prior to about 1945, Indiana Amish records were apparently kept mainly in family Bibles, whether written on the flyleafs or on notebook paper folded inside the pages.

The development since 1945 of a tradition of displaying family history records on the wall is symptom of a greater toleration by the Amish for all kinds of wall decorations (except those that depict the human form). Church rules regarding what may be displayed on interior walls vary from district to district. A good case in point is in Mifflin County, Pennsylvania, where an Amish family makes glass-painted family records that may not be hung on the walls of their own homes because of the church *Ordnung* (rules). In this regard, the Amish districts of Elkhart and LaGrange counties in Indiana are more liberal.

Another feature of Amish belief helps explain why the display of family records has such great appeal for many Amish. That is their literal interpretation of the Second Commandment which, since the Jakob Amman split (1693-97) from the Swiss Mennonites, has led them to forbid the depiction of the human form in art and which, in turn, has led modern Amish people to reject photography.

In a culture that forbids the taking of family pictures for posterity, the records shown here become treasured substitutes for photographs of infant births, marriage parties, family reunions, and aged forebears. Thus, although these records preserve only vital statistics, they contribute much more to the emotional and religious experience of belonging to an Amish family—indeed to the Amish faith.

Birth Records

The three birth records pictured here illustrate the technique of reverse painting on glass, using a foil background, as described in the preceding chapter.

Figure 1: Birth record for Daniel Glick. The birth record

(13 x 20 in.) for Daniel Glick continues an old tradition of making such records for people long after the birth itself. This one was made for Daniel in 1947, when he was 52 years old, by his wife Mary, who was a prolific glass painting artist near Topeka, Indiana. The Glicks were Amish when they lived in Iowa, but became Mennonites after moving to Indiana.

Figure 2: Birth record for Jewel Ann Miller. Although the birth record (6 x 9 in.) for Jewel Ann Miller of near Goshen was made in 1964, later than the Glick record, it actually illustrates much older design elements. Bird and card are indebted to the tradition of name cards decorated with elements of the Spencerian type of penmanship taught in American schoolrooms of the nineteenth and early twentieth centuries, and still admired and imitated by some older Amish writers. The record is "framed" with colored passepartout tape, as recommended by Thayer and Chandler, a crafts supply house in Chicago that popularized "Glorified Glass" painting in the 1930s.

Figure 3: Birth record for Glen Lehman. This birth record (10 x 13 in.) was made in 1982 near Middlebury. Its design shows affinities with recent commercial greeting card motifs. It is also a silent witness to the Amish reluctance to depict the human form, since the pattern from which this design was adapted had a baby's head sticking out of the bootie.

Marriage Records

Figure 4: Marriage record for Merlin and Mary Lehman. The foil painting in figure 4 represents the most common form and pattern for marriage records (sometimes called "holy matrimonies") in the Amish communities of northern Indiana. Circulating among Amish women since about 1945, it has been adapted to other media such as painted towels and other kinds of glass painting.

Figure 5: Lithographed marriage record. The lithographed marriage record (14.5 x 18.5 in.) upon which the design is based, was copyrighted in 1889 as "No. 14" by Meyer and Brother of Chicago. The foil painting version (17 x 21 in.), made in 1971, preserves almost all of the scriptural and factual text of the lithograph, but replaces the border and other decorations with bolder moral designs and changes the ovals to open books, presumably Bibles. Most important, the marriage record adds a list of twelve table-waiters at the bottom. The married couple's friends and relatives who serve the wedding meal are regarded as honored members of the bridal party and therefore included on the permanent record of the marriage. As noted in chapter 7, wedding records like this are sometimes prepared in advance of the wedding and first displayed on the wall behind the *Eck*, or corner table, where the wedding party sit for the wedding meal.

Figure 6: Marriage record for Wilson and Rosetta. This wedding record (18 x 23 in.) made near Nappanee for Wilson and Rosetta in 1985, uses a holographic poster, stuck-on letters, and styrofoam decorations, all purchased in stores. Only the frame is homemade. Since this record was presented to the parents of the newlyweds, it also serves the same function as the three-dimensional wedding souvenirs discussed next.

Wedding Favors

Customarily, the Amish bride and groom prepare personalized mementos of their wedding and give them to their parents and members of the wedding party. Usually three-dimensional, the wedding favors record the first names of the couple, the date of the wedding, and the names of the people to whom they are given. They are displayed in cupboards and on tables, just as wedding photographs would be in other cultures.

Figure 7: Wedding favors. Apparently the oldest form of such wedding records is the *stanga glas* (stemmed glass), which consists of a goblet holding various items. The earliest one I have seen was from 1909, near Shipshewana. It consists of a six-inch goblet with a colorful silk handkerchief draped over it. Originally, the goblet probably held a cookie with names and dates inscribed on it. The 15-inch *stanga glas* in the photo dates from 1976, which shows an amazing continuity in Amish

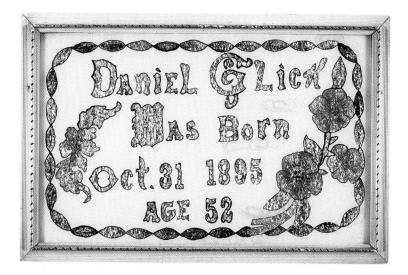

Figure 1. Birth record, Daniel Glick.

Figure 2. Birth record, Jewel Ann Miller.

Figure 3. Birth record for Glen Lehman.

Figure 4. Marriage record for Merlin and Mary Lehman.

Figure 6. Marriage record for Wilson and Rosetta.

Figure 5. Lithographed marriage record.

Figure 7. Wedding favors.

Figure 8. Howard Nisley family record.

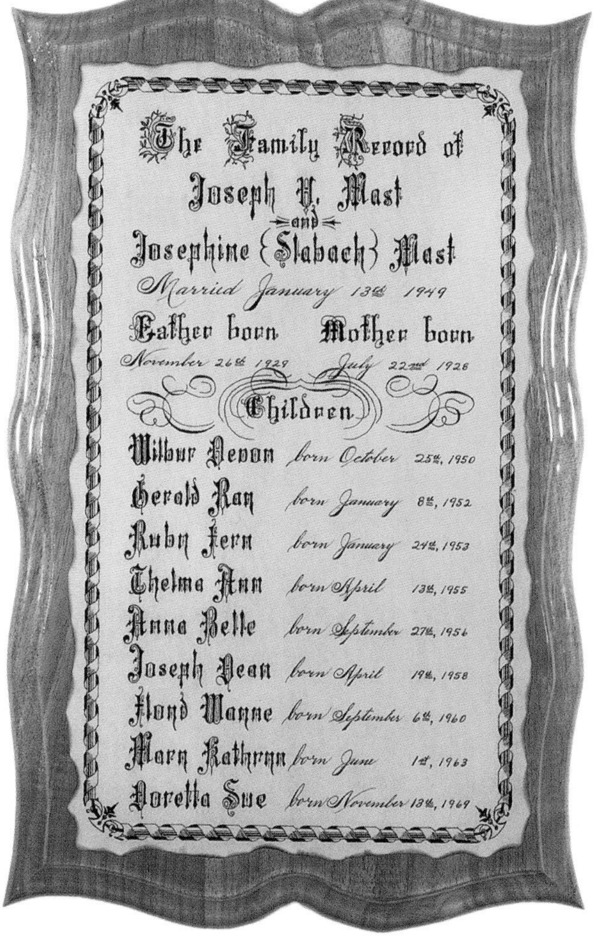

Figure 9. Joseph Mast family record.

Figure 10. Seth Troyer family record.

Figure 11. John Greenawalt family record.

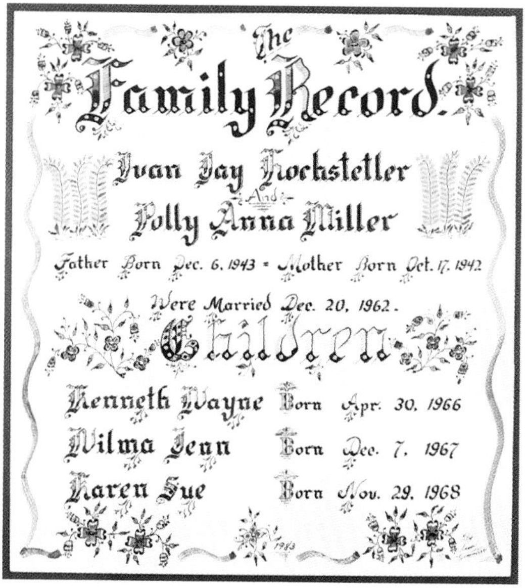

Figure 12. Ivan Hochstetler family record.

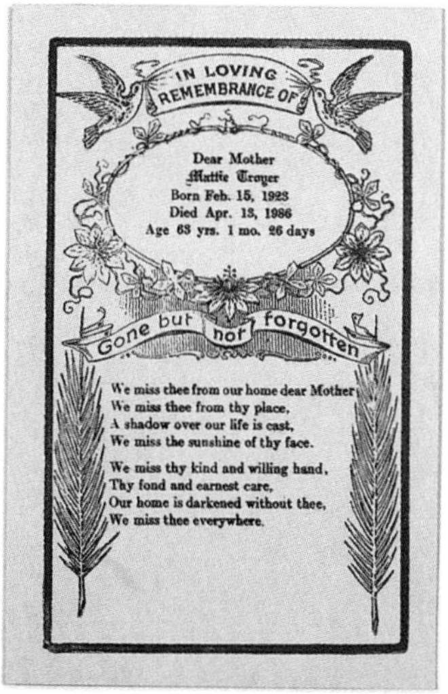

Figure 13. Memorial card.

Figure 14. Otto death record.

customs, despite styrofoam and other new elements. In recent years the forms that Amish wedding favors assume have multiplied, giving the impression that couples now try to create souvenirs that are as different as possible from those of previous couples. The two other favors in figure 7 are called "floats" or "trophies" by the Amish, since they bear some resemblance to floats that appear in parades and to trophies given as achievement awards (although not in Amish culture). The styrofoam Bible under the arch is dated November 6, 1975; the wooden float with open book and candle is dated May 3, 1984. Styrofoam parts to use in assembling wedding favors are available in Amish country stores. Amish woodworkers frequently have patterns for several different kinds of wooden floats that they can make, and adapt, upon demand.

Family Records

Figure 8: Howard Nisley family record. Most Amish family records (their name for genealogies) made today include only the vital statistics for two generations of a family—parents and children. The most common medium for family records is painting on glass. Many resemble the tinsel "Holy Matrimony" illustrated previously. The scroll-shaped record shown in figure 8 has lettering and design painted on top of the glass, with a colored background sprayed onto the backside. The glass is then "framed" with a ladder chain that grips all four sides and has a piece attached for suspending the record from a nail in the wall.

Figure 9: Joseph Mast family record. The tradition of fine penmanship lingers in some Amish family records. The Mast family record (11 x 17 in.) was done with pen and ink in 1982 by an Amish man from near Topeka, who learned Spencerian penmanship by studying manuals and corresponding with an older Amish calligrapher from Kansas who critiqued his work. For models of Gothic and other scripts, he consults a book of examples.

Figure 10: Seth Troyer family record. The Troyer family record (23 x 29 in.) was made in 1964 by Levi S. Troyer of near

Middlebury. Made with ballpoint pen and washed colored pencil, it features birds from the Spencerian tradition, angels from the fraktur tradition, and an overall design that the artist found in a family record form in the front of a Bible.

Although the Amish did not bring fraktur, as such, with them from Europe or Pennsylvania to Indiana, two records show a continuing interest in using that type of art for commemorative purposes.

Figure 11: John Greenawalt family record. The oldest family record known to me from the northern Indiana Amish community is the one made for John and Lydia Greenawalt c. 1867 by John's brother Christian C. of near Topeka. The design of the register area comes from a printed form published by Currier and Ives in 1852. The floral design, while related to fraktur work, is actually theorem art, which was popular in the United States during the early nineteenth century. Theorem art consists of an artistic arrangement of outline patterns that are then filled in with watercolors. The "hex" sign at bottom center, surmounted by paired birds and a one-stem tree of life, is all that remains of the Pennsylvania German folk inheritance of the Greenawalt family, which originated in Mifflin County, Pennsylvania. The other flowers, foliage, and birds are from mainstream American designs.

The large size (20 x 26 in.) and bright colors might, at first thought, seem unusual for an Amish record of so early a date. The Greenawalts were actually Amish Mennonites, meaning that they belonged to a large group of American Amish who eventually merged with the Mennonite Church, unlike the Old Order Amish who, during the period from 1850 to 1880, established a more rigid *Ordnung* (rules) and have since resisted acculturation and technological change to a much greater extent.

Figure 12: Ivan Hochstetler family record. The Hochstetler family record (16 x 20 in.) was made in 1983 by a middle-aged Amish man near Topeka. Done with speedwell ink, it is based on a design used by an Amish man from Gap, Pennsylvania.

Death Records

Figure 13: Memorial card. To commemorate the death of a loved one, Amish families usually order printed memorial cards from an Amish printer in Gordonville, Pennsylvania, the one shown in figure 13 (6.25 x 4.5 in.) being dated 1986. Such cards are often displayed behind the panes of glass-door cupboards in Amish homes.

Figure 14: Otto death record. The design of the printed memorial card has obviously influenced death records (sometimes called "loving memories") in other media, including this glass painting (11 x 14 in.). Made near Goshen in 1968, it adapts a foil painting design to a slightly different glass-painting technique. Like foil painting, all paint is applied to the back side of the glass; unlike tinsel painting, the sparkling effect comes from silver glitter glued to the glass, rather than from crinkled tinfoil between glass and backing. Since the painting needs no backing, it can be framed with ladder chain, like the family record shown earlier.

The Relief Sale Festival

"It still remains difficult to reconcile participation in festival with being a 'serious' person. . . . Traditional preindustrial people, of course, understand otherwise."
—*Richard Bauman*[1]

The Michiana Mennonite Relief Sale, held the fourth Saturday in September at the Elkhart County (Indiana) Fairgrounds in Goshen, does not (yet) appear among the 614 festivals listed in "Enjoy Indiana," a booklet published by the Indiana Department of Commerce, Division of Tourism. But many people who attend the relief sale have at least a hunch that it is more than a means of relieving human suffering sponsored by the Mennonite Central Committee (MCC). Some try to put the genius of the relief sale into words: "It's like a fair, except there are no rides. You buy things instead" (Benjamin Rohrer, 11 years, 1999).[2] "Coming here is like a very large family reunion" (Joan Hockman, 1999). "We're not here to make money. We're here to make people happy" (pie-seller, 1999). What these people sense—and what the folklorist knows—is that the Mennonite Relief Sale is also a folk festival. It is an unselfconscious expressive performance by Mennonites of their ethnic identity.[3] The relief sale, as festival, strengthens the Michiana Mennonite community as much as it relieves suffering in the wider world.

Definitions of "folk festival" by folklorists embrace what has taken place since 1966 at the Elkhart County Fairgrounds near Goshen, Indiana, every fourth Saturday in September: "[Festivals] occur at calendrically regulated intervals and are public in nature, participatory in ethos, complex in structure, and multiple in voice, scene, and purpose. Festivals are collective phenomena and serve purposes rooted in group life."[4] The relief sale, as festival, is "a community expression suspending the rules of everyday life." It "reaffirms the cohesion of a social group to its communitarian structure through participation in a time of revitalization," which is "cosmic" as well as social and cultural.[5]

The main difference between the relief sale and most festivals in the "Enjoy Indiana" list is that the relief sale is a "carnivalesque" festival, rather than a "folklorized" festival, to use Marianne Mesnil's terminology. Folklorized festivals often serve "the commercial, ideological, or political purposes of self-interested authorities or entrepreneurs."[6] However, the relief sale is a festival prepared "by the people for the people"[7]—not by the establishment for itself, or by the people for the establishment, or by the establishment for the people, or by the people versus the establishment.[8] Oddly, because Mennonites do not regard the relief sale as a festival, and in fact think they are engaged in an entirely other enterprise, the relief sale is a more "authentic" folk festival than if Mennonites folklorized it—that is, than if they self-consciously planned it as a festival.

Folklorized festivals emphasize performances for the entertainment of passive audiences. But the seeming chaos of the carnivalesque Mennonite relief sale results from the fact that all attendees are participants, not passive audience. Because the sale emphasizes purchasing things, everyone can participate as fully as they like. They can eat the pancakes and sausages. They can bid on quilts. They can "Run for Relief" in the five-kilometer contest. They can buy shoofly pie to take home. If a folklorized festival emphasizes "make-see," then the relief sale, as carnivalized festival, emphasizes "make-do"[9] since all in attendance contribute to the festive activities.

An overwhelming majority of the estimated 30,000 people who attend the Michiana relief sale, from Friday evening through Saturday afternoon, are Mennonites—which makes it an in-group festival. But since it is publicly advertised, strangers are also welcome and create some of the exotic element that "carnies" add to other kinds of festivals. Some visiting strangers are well-heeled urban tourists—from Detroit, Chicago, or Indianapolis—who come to look at the natives and to join the festive proceedings by buying quilts. Others are Mennonites from distant communities who have heard about the big sale by word of mouth and sometimes arrive in campers that they park on the fairgrounds for the duration. The worldwide crafts sold from the Ten Thousand Villages tables also bring a foreign, exotic element to the festival.

Although such widespread participation brings to festival behavior a sense of chaos, and although the various kinds of festivals in world cultures differ widely from each other, certain predictable events and sequences make up a kind of "morphology," or ritual structure, for the folklore genre of festival. I will blend insights from folklorists Beverly Stoeltje and Alessandro Falassi to discuss the archetypal festival elements found in the Michiana Mennonite Relief Sale: "rites" (to use Falassi's term) of valorization and devalorization, display, consumption, competition, and exchange.

Rites of Valorization and Devalorization

Festivals create a "time out of time"—a liminal experience—by claiming or re-claiming an otherwise ordinary time and space for the special carnivalesque needs of festival: "An area is reclaimed, cleared, delimited, blessed, adored, forbidden to normal activities."[10] Consequently, festivals are usually framed by opening events that "valorize" the holiday time and place and by concluding events that "devalorize" it and return it and the participants to an everyday time and place.

For the Michiana relief sale, valorizing means sacralizing the otherwise secular Elkhart County Fairgrounds. Especially for the more conservative Mennonite-related groups, as well as for older Mennonites who recall that attendance at county fairs used to be forbidden, sacralizing the fairgrounds is an important step. However, that task has been more easily accomplished since the 1980s, when the local relief sale board paid for and, with volunteers, built the large fairgrounds building that now houses the quilt auction. Nowadays, in sacralizing the fairgrounds, Mennonites are, in effect, re-claiming the building that was once their own.

Valorization occurs most obviously in the opening program of the sale, the Friday evening worship service in the quilt building. In recent years, the program in the early part of the evening has featured a "sacred concert" by the inter-congregational MCC Relief Sale Men's Chorus. In 1999, the program theme was "Healer of Our Every Ill," which called attention to the world needs that the sale responds to. The event opened with a welcome by the sale's vice-president, then a prayer that emphasized not the needs of the world but the need for Mennonites to "come together as a community." Choir and audience then sang "606," the Mennonite ethnic anthem, prior to the choir concert.[11] In 2002, the choir concluded their program with "606," although then the audience itself sang it again—standing spontaneously—following which, all applauded each other in an affirmation of tribal solidarity.

However, this program—with its official, decorous content and intention—was so often disrupted by sale-goers milling around on the edges of the large meeting, especially to look at the quilts in their maze of racks, that some men were posted on the fringes of the crowd, holding large printed signs that read: "Please be quiet. Thank you."

The meaning of the sale is again valorized the next day at 8 a.m. in the quilt building, when the first two items auctioned off are loaves of whole wheat bread (selling for $200 a loaf in 1999). The auctioning of the bread becomes a ritualistic symbol both of the worldwide need for basic food and of communion by sale-goers with each other as well as with the needy.

During the choir program on opening night of the Michiana Mennonite Relief Sale the bustling crowd is admonished to "Please Be Quiet."

Valorization occurs most dramatically at noon, when the quilt sale stops, the audience is quieted and someone leads in the singing of a hymn and someone else offers a prayer—not to bless the food eaten but to invoke the values of the sale.

The "official" valorizing motive for the sale is reinforced by the Mennonite Central Committee's information booth, located in a tent or building in a prime location on the grounds and offering information on MCC and the Mennonite Church through videotapes, printed materials, displays, and well informed interpreters. Although the MCC booth is intended to orient strangers to those subjects, it seems to attract visits mainly by persons who have had or would like to have assignments with MCC.

So that sale-goers would not forget what should motivate their behavior, valorizing signs used to be posted in the various areas of the sale, stating such Christian admonitions as:

Feeding the hungry.

Blessed are the peacemakers,
for they shall be called the sons of God.

If someone strikes you on the right cheek,
turn to him the other one.

God is love. Whoever lives in love, lives in God,
and God in him.

The serious contents of those signs, in 1982, jostled with the festive activity that surrounded them.

Valorization occurs behind the scenes, too. A relief sale "kick-off" supper and program is held in the spring of each year, open to the public but intended to launch work on the year's sale and inspire midlevel administrators. In 2002 the event was held on April 25 at Clinton Frame Mennonite Church in rural Goshen and included a devotional by pastor Terry Diener, who spoke about his MCC service in Brazil, and a longer talk by Rick Hostetler, medical doctor, on his recent visit to Iraq on behalf of MCC.

The official reason, or sanction, for the relief sale festival is presented more often and more intensively than is usually the case at festivals. On one level, that is because the sale has a basically religious motivation. As one organizer emphasized at Clinton Frame, it's "not just food and quilts!" If organizers of the sale "protest too much," it may be because some elements of festival—as with the milling crowds during the Friday worship service, and other features to be described below—threaten to overwhelm the stated reason for the event.

As with most festivals, the devalorization of the relief sale occurs in a modest, low-ritual way: at the end of the quilt auction a prayer is offered, people are thanked, and the quilt building reverts to being just another empty fairgrounds building. Elsewhere, roughly simultaneous with the quilt sale, the festival dwindles gradually and anti-climactically, as one activity after another closes down, chairs and equipment are put away, and litter is cleared up, beginning about 3 p.m.

De-valorizing used to culminate the following day in Sunday worship services in local congregations, when out-of-town visitors to the sale were acknowledged and welcomed and the total proceeds of the sale were announced—usually to the audible approval of worshipers. Many congregations have done away with that too-materialistic, too-festive moment. Nowadays, the final event is an informal meeting of sale officers and board members on the Monday following the sale. It is a kind of debriefing session, mainly with stories and accounts of "how the sale went" in areas and activities that administrators were unable to visit. A one-page financial report concludes the annual relief sale cycle.

Rites of Conspicuous Display

Festivals typically feature parades or other processional presentations of items that express the sponsoring community's identity or self-image, and some festivals elevate and exhibit individuals—the homecoming king or queen, the grand marshall, the holiday saint—who temporarily embody the community's best values.[12] Neither kind of display is literally found at the relief sale. Even the winner of the Run for Relief goes virtually unheralded—and wins only a pie. The closest one gets to "procession" is the line for the sausage and pancake breakfast that slowly wends its way into the dark tent. The closest one gets to king or queen of the sale are the people (mostly women) who preside over the quilt auction and the auctioneers (mostly men) who work in the several auctions. The auctioneers are rendered especially conspicuous by their costume, many being dressed in coats and ties and some in cowboy hats and boots and bright coats. Serious quilt-buyers also go on conspicuous display by paying to obtain prime seats in the first few rows of the quilt sale building.

Of course, the dominant "conspicuous display" of the relief

sale is of the commodities offered for sale. In fact, the main appeal of the Friday night program is to let the next day's sale-goers get a preliminary survey of items for sale, so that they can be at the right place at the right time on Saturday. Most elaborately displayed are the quilts, in their labyrinth of racks, carefully numbered and tabulated—the touring of which establishes its own very elaborate in-and-out, snakelike procession. The same element of display can be found, to a lesser degree, in the buildings that house the crafts and the three other auctions.

Rites of Conspicuous Consumption

Festival-goers not only display their identity, they also ingest it—heartily.[13] However, unlike at most festivals, no alcoholic drinks are consumed at the Mennonite relief sale. The "conspicuous consumption" consists of food. And more food. In 2001, the 50 different food stands earned about $130,000, or 35 percent of total sale proceeds. In 1999, 25,000 apple fritters were sold. Eighty-two donated hogs were butchered to make

Apple fritters are one of the favorite foods at the relief sale.

sausage, headcheese, scrapple, and pork sandwiches. And sale-goers consumed 2,000 halves of Nelson's Golden Glo chicken.

Certain foods are consumed by sale-goers mainly—or only—at the relief sale and therefore constitute "festival" foods. The more exotic ones are funnel cakes, rosettes, elephant ears, and half-moon pies, none of which have been traditional foods of widespread use in Michiana Mennonite homes. As with festival foods in general, many foods that used to be everyday foods, especially in rural Mennonite households, are now consumed only once a year, at the relief sale, because the Mennonite economy and culture have changed so much. These festival foods include sausage and pancakes for breakfast, mush, headcheese, scrapple, shoofly pie, apple fritters, and apple butter (which continues to be homemade on the sale grounds). The sausage consumed at the sale probably represents the most direct connection with Mennonites' European origins, since it is locally made according to a traditional family recipe maintained by the Mishler family.

The changing nature of the Mennonite community, as revealed by foods, includes the presence in recent years of a few non-European food stands, namely eggrolls (from the influence of Asian refugees) and Mexican food items (from the growing Hispanic Mennonite Church in northern Indiana). Even *pluma moos*, representing Russian Mennonite culture, has been added to the menu in recent years. In light of some Mennonites' diet consciousness, some stands now offer salads, fruits, and diet drinks. But they are "for the fanatical" and take "all the fun out of it" (Andrea Zuercher, 1982). "It has to be fattening [made with lard] to be good, you know," said one pie-seller in 1999.

The sale puts so much emphasis on the preparing, buying, and eating of food that official sale sponsors try hard to squelch the tendency of sale-goers to reinterpret in a perverse way the motto of the Michiana Mennonite Relief Sale: "Dedicated to feeding the hungry in the name of Jesus Christ." A second meaning of "feeding the hungry" refers to sale-goers' own indulgence as they graze on goodies from building to building, booth to booth. "This is the Mennonite FOOD sale" (shortcake seller 1999). "This is pig-out day" (woman in pancake line 1999). "I begin at one gate and eat my way through the camp, then start back" (Martha Liechty Conrad, 1984). "I consumed two eggrolls, a kneepatch, an apple fritter, a dish of strawberry shortcake, a sausage sandwich, and two glasses of orange drink and bought a roll of bologna to take home" (Twila Yoder, 1982).

"Feeding the hungry" becomes a joking proverbial saying in many conversational exchanges. Other variants include:

"Eating to help the starving." (John Liechty, 1982)

"Boy, that guy's *really* dedicated to feeding the hungry." (Randy Jacobs, 1982)

"Get fat for Jesus." (Karl Shelley)

The grim paradox of rich Americans stuffing themselves in order to contribute money for food relief troubles some sale organizers. In 1991, MCC, for instance, formulated an expanded mission statement for relief sales that avoids the word "feeding" altogether: "This sale is dedicated to helping the hungry, homeless, war-torn, sick, handicapped, jobless, and illiterate around the world in the name of Jesus Christ." However, the shorter statement, "Dedicated to feeding the hungry in the name of Jesus Christ," remains the one used by the Michiana sale committee on its brochure and on the banner that hangs above the quilt auction.

Rites of Competition

Festivals offer participants the thrill of observing and, better yet, participating in contests and competitions that serve to encourage skills associated with the community's everyday work and to reaffirm the group's important values.[14] The literal competitions in the relief sale are minor events that attract little attention and involve few participants: the five-kilometer "Run for Relief" and the three-on-three basketball tournament.

The true competition of the sale—its agon, or drama—resides in the four auctions: of quilts, of miscellaneous new and used items, of antiques, and of items for children. The most important competition is the quilt auction, which contributed $151,220 (41 percent) of the total proceeds in 2001. The quilt auction so dominates the event that, as far as the Elkhart County Convention and Visitors Bureau is concerned, the day is "The Quilt Auction" rather than the "Michiana Mennonite Relief Sale."[15]

The quilt auction is a democratic competition, since any one person in the audience of over 1500 people may compete for a quilt, or for paying the highest price for a quilt, or for buying the designated "sale" quilt of unique design. In 1999 when 364 items were auctioned, there were 364 different scenes of competition between 8 a.m. to 4 p.m. (about 46 per hour), some short and quiet but others—the ones the crowd waits for—being very dramatic indeed. The skilled auctioneer gradually becomes more intense and persuasive, and his "spotters" range up and down the six aisles, gesturing broadly and shouting out loudly the bids they receive. "Duane Troyer of Goshen, Indiana, the most flamboyant of all aisle auctioneers . . . [was] kneeling with bidders, putting his arm around them, sitting beside them and always making eye contact, which had the effect of pressuring the audience" (Tim Kennel and Andre King, 1999). The final "Sold!" sometimes brings laughter, cheers and applause from the audience and smiles of triumph from the auctioneer and his cohorts. It is a cathartic experience, in a kind of impromptu comedy, for all concerned. That kind of dramatic competition is repeated hundreds of additional times, usually in a more muted way, in the other three auctions.

More subtle competition occurs behind the scenes of the sale. Individual food stalls compete with their neighbors for higher total proceeds, and even with themselves from one year to another. Each sale, in effect, is in competition to exceed all previous sales in total income—and indeed until 1999 that was the case, with each sale yielding an ever-increasing total. Now that sale proceeds have begun to taper off—total sales peaked in 1999, but total proceeds for MCC had peaked already in

Auctioneers and bid-takers volunteer their services at the antiques auction.

1992—the sense of competition has becomes more grim and less is made of total income than used to be the case. Finally, one area relief sale competes with other, more distant area sales for the largest proceeds, with the Michiana sale being one of the top three in North America in net income.

Rites of Exchange

One major outcome of festival is the exchange, or redistribution, of wealth. Insofar as festivals repay "the community or the gods for what [has been] received in excess,"[16] this important feature distinguishes the Mennonite relief sale from most other festivals.

The redistribution occurs on two levels. First, of course, the main goal of the festival is to redistribute the world's resources—taking money from middle-class people in mid-north-central Indiana to needy people throughout the world.

A second redistribution—or perhaps re-definition—of wealth also occurs within the sponsoring Mennonite community. The poor members of the church contribute a lot of work and time, some materials and a lesser amount of cash. The wealthy members of the church contribute excessive amounts of cash: $200 for a loaf of bread, $1,500 for a marble roller, $7,000 for a quilt. As one non-Mennonite said in the quilt tent, upon seeing a quilt sold for $6,700: "This is a millionaire's hall." And as one quilter with talent but little cash said, "I can make them for myself . . . for less than I would pay for one here. The ones buying them have lots of money" (Mary Shafer, 1984). "Bid with your heart," says the sale brochure. In 2001, $310,000 left Indiana coffers and went to the needy world; at the peak of the sale's success in 1999, $440,000 of excess was redistributed.

Rites of Reversal or Extension?

A continuing issue in the study of festival behavior by anthropologists and folklorists is whether a festival constitutes a *reversal* of the everyday behavior and values of the participants (as in the New Orleans Mardi Gras) or an *extension* of everyday behavior and values. The Mennonite relief sale does illustrate some radical shifting of the Mennonite community's priorities and hierarchies, thereby fulfilling Victor Turner's claim that festival is a time when people are allowed to violate everyday norms.[17]

Perhaps the most immediately obvious reversal is in attitude toward getting and spending. At the relief sale otherwise frugal, simple-living Mennonites spend their money with abandon— often for things they do not really need. As one non-Mennonite put it, "On this day these people who are known for their frugalness can't seem to part with their money fast enough" (Ginger Miller, 1982). And as one auctioneer encouraged his audience in 2002: "It's only money. You can't take it with you, so spend away!" If carnival is a "time out of time" that sanctions extraordinary behavior, this fiscal abandonment is most impressive, even if it is "for a good cause."

Gender roles also undergo reversal at the sale. The relief sale is a predominantly women's operation. Women, supervised by other women, prepare the quilts, food, and handicrafts that accounted for seventy-nine percent of the sale's proceeds in 2001.[18] On the day of the sale they are publicly prominent, since they present the quilts in the big auction, they stand behind the handicrafts for sale, and they dominate most of the food stalls. However, such gender reversal must be qualified with some persisting evidences of traditional Mennonite patriarchy. The opening program Friday night establishes the norms for the community and the sale by offering a very traditional men's chorus and other leadership by men, with women being virtually absent from the stage. The male auctioneers ultimately dominate and control the quilt sale. And, oddly, men decidedly dominate in preparing and serving the pancake and sausage breakfast—the largest food sale—as well as in some other food stalls. Perhaps this latter kind of gender reversal—men displacing women—helps compensate to some degree for the reversal accomplished more impressively by women elsewhere in the sale.

The sale also reverses the hierarchies of the clergy and the laity and the intellectuals and the less well educated. Mennonite Church affairs have traditionally been directed and dominated by ministers, who are definitely not in leadership positions at the relief sale, and some of whom are even displeased by the time and effort their members give to it. And if intellectuals conduct the affairs of the Mennonite Church at large, they do not dominate the relief sale, which tends—also like Mennonite Disaster Service and MCC meat-canning—to rely more on grassroots laborers than on persons with advanced degrees. In fact, well educated Mennonites tend to stay at home and criticize the relief sale on theological grounds.[19]

In addition to raising money, how do Mennonites benefit from the festival experience that the relief sale offers? If the relief sale is essentially a "reversal" of everyday life, then it yields to the analysis of functional anthropologists who, following Freud, see such festivals as being therapeutic for their participants. That is, participating in rituals of reversal enables otherwise oppressed festival-goers to experience a temporary release, or escape, that makes it possible for them to return the next day—oppositional feelings defused—to their normal activity. Their culture remains unchanged and festival thereby conserves tradition by allowing people to harmlessly experience its opposite values. Victor Turner gives this temporary reprieve a more positive interpretation by claiming that the *communitas*, or democratic leveling, that occurs during the festival temporarily attains the higher political values of the community that sponsors it, even though during the rest of the year they submit to the hierarchies required by practical survival.[20]

From a less deterministic perspective, especially that of the Christian cultural theorist Mikhail Bakhtin, carnival's ritual of reversal—even though it exists for only a short time—does, by degrees and over time, subvert, critique, and transform the everyday culture in the direction of the reversed culture that temporarily exists during the festival.[21] It is interesting to notice that during the forty-odd years of the relief sale's history, Mennonite churches have indeed tended to evolve in the direction of the reversals noted above: Mennonites have become more prosperous and less frugal, Mennonite women have gained in equality with men, and the laity's participation in and direction of church affairs has increased. If the relief sale has not helped bring about those changes, it at least mirrors them.

I personally think it is more important to see the relief sale as not mainly a reversal but as a natural extension, writ large, of many "festivities" that Mennonites have traditionally—and still do—sponsor and participate in. The most obvious connection is with the household auction, which constitutes a practical Saturday entertainment for many Mennonites and Amish and also often includes homemade food served as a benefit for a parochial school or a family in need. The relief sale thus continues to dignify the folk skill of auctioneering, which always been one of three public performance skills sanctioned by Mennonite and Amish communities—the others being preaching and song leading.

The decline in MCC relief sale revenue may be a sign of the sale's success, not its failure. One reason for its recent decline is the number of other charity auctions that Mennonite and other church groups in Michiana have begun to sponsor: for Haiti relief (which attracts Old Order Amish and other conservative groups away from the MCC relief sale), for the Goldenrod Community, for Bethany and Clinton Christian High Schools, and for individual Amish families suffering from catastrophic health care costs. How many quilts can Mennonite and Amish quilters make in trying to support all of these sales? Each such spin-off auction testifies to the thriving health of such folk festivals in Michiana. The relief sale has served to re-invigorate the auction as a festive tradition within Mennonite communities.

The relief sale is also an extension of the barn-raising bee, in the form of the "Shalom" house often built by men prior to the sale, with all proceeds from the sale of the house going to MCC. Quilts and other handicrafts are extensions of Mennonite women's "sewing circles," which have always been associated with local and world relief efforts. The quilt auction has certainly revived and even expanded the folk art of quilting in Mennonite circles. The food resembles a giant potluck, offering foods that Swiss Mennonites in the U.S. have traditionally preferred. And in being a gathering of the Mennonite community the relief sale becomes a glorified family, or denominational, reunion.

Finally, its calendric location near the end of September associates it with the universal phenomenon of the harvest festival.[22] Of course, it is not literally so—except perhaps in some of the seasonal foods offered for sale, such as molasses, apple butter, apple fritters, ground cherries, and the "harvest" of fattened pigs (usually butchered in the winter). But the celebration of excess that the sale emphasizes and the erstwhile agricultural life that Mennonites have lived do turn it into a recognizable harvest festival.

Folk customs, including festivals, are performances of identity, that is, the traditional physical practices of social groups express deeply held values and convictions that are given embodied form in festival activity. As publicly expressed by the relief sale, Mennonite ethnic identity includes such traits as generosity, hard work, organizational skills and cooperation, practical technical expertise, modesty in self-display, plain aesthetic (in the sale itself, not the quilts and other crafts), communal association, a service ethic, self-sacrifice, concern for the needs of the wider world. Or as Dan Beachy, a former president of the Michiana relief sale, put it more succinctly: the sale shows that Mennonites are "industrious, honest, faithful, communal."[23]

The relief sale may critique and transform Mennonite culture, but it most obviously extends and enlarges traditional activities and attitudes in order to re-affirm and celebrate essentials of Mennonite identity, especially at a time when the community is coping with rapid change and increasing diversity.

Official and Unofficial Culture at the Relief Sale

One thumbnail definition of folklore is "unofficial culture," meaning aspects of culture that are based on unspoken but commonly held values, whether or not those values are also articulated by authorities who control official hierarchies in a community.

Some elements of the relief sale discussed previously, such as the disruption of the Friday night choral program, point to a subversion of the officially announced norms of the sale. In this regard, the relief sale festival becomes "the people vs. the establishment." The playful re-interpretation of "feeding the hungry" is a prime example of the folk asserting their own value in opposition to official pronouncements, as festival-goers pay more attention to feeding themselves than to feeding the destitute of the world.

Run for Relief has also assumed a subversive proverbial meaning. Its scatological connotation is best captured by this anecdote:

> I was in the quilt auction tent when they switched auctioneers. The new man was apparently recently elected for the

auctioneers' hall of fame. Here's what he said as soon as he got to the mike and before he started auctioning: "There's lots of hungry people in the world . . . and as I found out this morning, also lots of hungry people here at the sale. [Audience laughs.] I had to wait in line for an hour this morning for my pancakes and sausage, only to find out in the end that it was the line for the ladies' restroom. [More laughter.] Maybe that's why they call it a 'relief' auction. [Audience in uproar.]" (Tim Manickam, 1982)

In re-interpreting those two proverbs, "feeding the hungry" and "run for relief," sale-goers assert festival norms in opposition to the official value placed on the sale by organizers.

Actually, from the time of the earliest sales, thoughtful leaders have perceived certain endemic "problems" with the relief sale, springing from the difficulty of rationalizing actual behavior with stated norms. The persistent problems have to do with (1) eating so others may be fed and (2) contributing money but expecting merchandise in return. The more recently articulated problem concerns (3) the sale's failure to reach non-Mennonite audiences.[24] An interesting response to the first two problems can be found in a feature article that John Bender, on behalf of the Michiana sale committee, wrote about the relief sale for the *South Bend Tribune* in 1979.[25]

Bender said that the first problem, of "over-eating so that others may be fed," constitutes a "paradox at best," since the two actions are "mutually exclusive." Although he cites the connection of the sale to the well-supplied tables, pantries, and smokehouses of traditional Mennonite households, he cannot resolve the contradiction. Accepting that sale-time indulgence in fattening food is wrong, he defends Mennonites by citing their emergent discussions of wellness and ecology. He also cites the *More-with-Less Cookbook* (1976), which was derived from author Doris Janzen Longacre's experience with MCC and which shows how to eat well and deplete fewer of the world's resources.[26]

Nor can Bender resolve the second problem—that Mennonites seem to be able to give money to MCC, not by making an outright voluntary contribution but only by selfishly obtaining quilts, rosettes, or marble rollers in return. Bender sidesteps the issue by saying that, after all, money is not the essence of the relief sale, the *attitude* of service is: "What makes a relief sale tick is not money but people willingly giving themselves and their time." Even the quilts have value only insofar as they represent "the interest of a service rendered and the satisfaction of a skill put to use." Finally, Bender quotes an official statement by MCC: "Relief and service have validity for us only as the motivation, spirit, and methods of work are in keeping with the Bible." Hence, Bender ignores the hard materiality of the relief sale—the juicy sausage, the Carolina Lily quilts, the $440,000—in favor of abstract, essentialist ideas *about* the sale, which the average sale-goer might agree with, upon reflection, although not by behavior at the sale.

Bender's attempt to rationalize festival activity fulfills the quotation from Richard Bauman at the beginning of this essay, which stresses the puritan notion that carnivalesque indulgence does not characterize "serious" people. Mennonite intellectuals and administrators clearly tend to be uncomfortable with the carnality of the relief festival.

The third problem—that the sale appeals mainly to Mennonites rather than outsiders—has both a practical and a theological side. As sale revenues decline, sales need to reach new audiences in order to generate more income. And in order for sales also to communicate Mennonite values to others, they need to be made to appeal to more than members of an ethnic in-group. Recently, therefore, MCC consultants have been encouraging local sale committees to respond to these new realities. The southwest Pennsylvania relief sale—serving the geographic corner formed by the boundaries of Pennsylvania, Maryland, and West Virginia—has responded in two ways: by moving the sale away from the Mennonite community to a fairgrounds near a non-Mennonite resort area, and by offering more performer-audience programming. Their revenue has increased by thirty percent.[27] Encouraged by MCC, some sale organizers—especially in the western U.S. and Canada—increasingly regard and plan the sale as a "festival," even to the point of using "festival" as part of the name for the relief sales in Oregon, southern California, Winnipeg, and Central Fraser Valley (British Columbia). For the 2002 sales throughout Canada and the U.S., MCC tried to strengthen the witnessing aspect of the sale by suggesting that each sale stress the motto, "Come, follow me," as an evangelical invitation consonant with the "missional" vision of the newly merged Mennonite Church.

Both impulses—to "improve" the sale by resisting its carnality and to turn it into a more "folklorized" festival that presents programs for a public audience—certainly threaten the relief sale's current nature and function and perhaps its very continuing existence. Such reforms threaten to domesticate the event and turn it into a more calculated performance that will present Mennonites as they *think* they are, or as they *want* to be, rather than as they *really are*.

The genius of Mennonite relief sales is that they have not been subject to official control "from above," as it were. Relief sales originated in a Morgantown, Pennsylvania, barnyard in 1957 and have since then grown abundantly—but with little direction from MCC officials in Akron, Pennsylvania. All of the forty-six sales throughout the U.S. and Canada are under full local control—no MCC directives guide them. MCC even allows local committees to designate to what worthy project the proceeds of their local sale should go.

In recent years, however, the "Resource Generation" staff at MCC-Akron has made more gestures toward unifying the work of local committees. Since 1997 there has been a North American Relief Sale Board, consisting of five regional representatives and led by "coordinators" on half-time salary from MCC. The board and coordinators have begun to sponsor international (U.S. and Canada) meetings of representatives of local relief sales committees, both for encouragement and for exchanging ideas and information. A recent suggestion emanating from MCC is that relief sales provide more self-consciously designed "festival" activities, such as demonstrations, storytelling programs, etc. Such programming, especially for a non-Mennonite audience, threatens to change the relief sale from a carnivalesque event for a close-knit community into a more pretentious, performance oriented, folklorized event for outsiders.

It may not be possible to resolve the paradoxes found in relief sales by enlightened Mennonites. After all, relief sales are like the ocean—they are there, probably not easily changed, and perhaps even indestructible. Selling food and quilts to raise money for world relief is inherent in this very successful Mennonite communal endeavor. The sale is best justified and rationalized for what it is—an ethnic festival—not for what it should be, according to official thinking.

Recent postmodern and feminist thinking about the body, about embodiment and about the materiality of human life is also important for any interpretation of relief sale activity. In recent years *The Mennonite Quarterly Review* has published important essays by Rudy Wiebe, Julia Kasdorf, Beth Martin Birky, and Pamela Classen[28] on how "the body knows," as Wiebe put it. Classen's work is directly relevant to theologizing the relief sale as festival, since she points out that Mennonite women, although traditionally barred from implementing the official worship rituals of the church upstairs, nevertheless performed corresponding rituals with food downstairs in order to sustain both the human body and the body of Christ, the church.

The word *carnival*, of course, derives from the Latin *carne*, a word that means "flesh" and the meaning of which was dignified most significantly for Christians in the *Incarnation*—the Word become Flesh. The relief sale as festival, specifically "carnivalesque" festivity, legitimately exploits the fleshly, physical, carnal body and material existence of everyone who participates. As folklorist Erin Roth points out, there is a kind of appropriateness in using (Mennonite) *material culture* at one end of the conduit (in Goshen) to generate *material aid* at the other end (Afghanistan).[29]

Furthermore, folklorists and anthropologists agree that the rationalization of faith and practice that occurred with the Reformation also split off *festival* from *worship* in Protestant cultures.[30] Iconoclastic, puritanical groups like Quakers and Anabaptists created the greatest divides between festival and religious ritual behavior, both by prohibiting festivals, in general, and by not regarding as particularly religious the festivities that are a part of their culture—auctions, barn-raisings, family reunions, and now relief sales. Since Mennonites have been deprived of church-sponsored festivals for almost 500 years, it is not surprising that they are loath to abandon or change the very successful one that they have recently developed.

The relief sale in Mennonite culture is certainly not a worship service, but its connection with explicit and implicit Mennonite norms helps bridge the historical schism of festival and ritual, brings the body back into Anabaptist theology and—if only for eight hours a year—integrates body and soul, individual and community in service "in the name of Christ."

Notes

Preface
1. Of course, it is never that simple. The three spheres of culture overlap. Items move from one sphere to another. The most important distinguishing factor is the mode of transmission: authoritative, formal means for academic culture; commercial mass media for popular culture; and informal/oral means for folk culture. See Jan Brunvand, *The Study of American Folklore*, 4th ed. (New York: Norton, 1998), 8-10.
2. Alan Dundes, "What Is Folklore?" in *The Study of Folklore*, ed. Alan Dundes (Englewood Cliffs, N.J.: Prentice-Hall, 1965), 2. For a complex discussion of what constitutes a folk group see Dorothy Noyes, "Group," *Journal of American Folklore* 108 (Fall 1995), 449-78.
3. The first completed volume is Alemu Checole, *Global Mennonite History: Volume One, Africa* (Waterloo, Ont.: Pandora Press, 2003).
4. Ervin Beck, "Telling the Tale in Belize," *Journal of American Folklore* 93 (Oct.-Dec. 1980), 417-34.
5. Daniel Ben-Amos, "Contextual Approach," in *American Folklore: An Encyclopedia,* ed. Jan Brunvand (New York: Garland, 1996), 158-59.

Chapter 1: Stories and Functions
1. William Bascom, "Four Functions of Folklore," *Journal of American Folklore* 67 (1954), 333-49.
2. Unless otherwise noted, the stories given here and elsewhere in *MennoFolk* come from oral tellings that have been transcribed and slightly edited for readability. Transcriptions and full attributions will be found in the Ervin Beck files of the Mennonite Church USA Archives, Goshen, Indiana.
3. Peter Jansz Twisck, *Downfall of the Tyrants, and Annual Events* [1620], in *The Complete Works of Menno Simons*, trans. John F. Funk (Elkhart, Ind.: J. F. Funk and Brother, 1871), Part 1, 451-52.
4. Alan Dundes, "The Functions of Folklore" in *The Study of Folklore*, ed. Alan Dundes (Englewood Cliffs, N.J.: Prentice-Hall, 1965), 277-78.

5. Elliott Oring, "Three Functions of Folklore: Traditional Functionalism as Explanation in Folkloristics," *Journal of American Folklore* 89 (1976), 67-80.

Chapter 2: Inter-Mennonite Ethnic Slurs

1. Don Yoder, "Pennsylvania Germans," *The Harvard Encyclopedia of American Ethnic Groups,* ed. Stephan Thernstrom (Cambridge: Harvard University Press, 1980), 770-72.

2. William Hugh Jansen, "The Exoteric-Esoteric Factor in Folklore," *Fabula: Journal of Folktale Studies* 2 (1959), 205-11.

3. Brethren people tell this story specifically about their elder Rufus P. Bucher (1883-1956) of southeastern Pennsylvania. Soon after Bucher died the story appeared in print, told about him, in *History of the Church of the Brethren, Eastern Pennsylvania,* ed. [Guy R. Saylor] (Church of the Brethren Eastern District of Pennsylvania, 1965), 270-71. John Ruth tells the story about a Brethren person in *A Quiet and Peaceable Life* (Intercourse, Pa.: Good Books, 1985), 62. More recently, ethicist Stanley Hauerwas tells it as an encounter between an Old Order Amish man and a tourist in Shipshewana, Indiana: e-mail from Steve Nolt, Goshen, Indiana, March 3, 2004.

4. Alan Dundes discusses the "international" nature of this riddle joke, meaning that it is told throughout the world, with different ethnic groups being named in the two "slots" of the joke. For instance, a version collected in Belgium in 1970 goes: "Why do the Americans have the Negroes and the Belgians have the Flemish? Because the Americans had first choice." Probably variants of most of the jokes considered in this chapter circulate among different groups and refer to ethnic groups other than Amish and Mennonites. However, no attempt will be made to document such diffusion: Alan Dundes, "Ethnicity and National Character" in *Cracking Jokes: Studies of Sick Humor Cycles and Stereotypes* (Berkeley, Calif.: Ten Speed Press, 1987), 100.

5. Donald B. Kraybill and C. Nelson Hostetler, *Anabaptist World USA* (Scottdale, Pa.: Herald Press, 2001), 144-46.

6. For full discussion of the attributes of all of these groups, see their entries in *The Mennonite Encyclopedia* (4 vols. + supp.) (Scottdale, Pa.: Mennonite Publishing House, 1955-59, 1990).

7. For additional readings on ethnic slurs, see Dundes, *Cracking Jokes,* chaps. 4-13; Andrea Greenberg, "Form and Function of the Ethnic Joke," *Keystone Folklore Quarterly* 17 (Winter 1972), 144-61; Christie Davies, *Ethnic Humor around the World* (Bloomington, Ind.: Indiana University Press, 1990).

Chapter 3: Origin Tales and Beliefs

1. The folklore genre of "legend" can be divided into four subgenres: etiological and eschatological legends; historical legends and legends of the history of civilization; supernatural beings and forces or mythical legends; and religious legends or myths of gods and heroes. See Linda Degh, "Folk Narrative," in *Folklore and Folklife, an Introduction,* ed. Richard M. Dorson (Chicago: University of Chicago Press, 1972), 53-84. To Degh's list of classic legend types need to be added legends of more recent identification and study, such as the urban legend (chapter 5) and the personal experience story. The term "etiological belief" is my own.

2. Roger D. Abrahams, *Afro-American Folk Tales: Stories from Black Traditions in the New World* (New York: Pantheon Books, 1985), 119-20, 207-09.

3. Judy Trejo, "Coyote Tales: A Paiute Commentary," *Journal of American Folklore* 87 (1974), 66-71.

4. "Anansi was originally a creator of the world in Gold Cost mythology": "Anansi," *Funk and Wagnalls Standard Dictionary of Folklore, Mythology and Legend,* Vol. 1 (New York: Funk and Wagnalls, 1949-50), 52.

5. Insofar as some items in this study are origin beliefs held by outsiders about Old Order Amish people, they offer additional evidence to support David Weaver-Zercher's analysis of how outsiders use the Amish to serve their own needs and purposes. See Zercher's *The Amish in the American Imagination* (Baltimore: Johns Hopkins University Press, 2001).

6. "The Esoteric-Exoteric Factor in Folklore," *Fabula* 2 (1959), 205-11.

7. Alfred L. Shoemaker discusses this belief in *Three Myths about the Pennsylvania Dutch Country* (Lancaster: Franklin and Marshall College, c. 1951), 29. He also devotes fifteen pages to exposing the popular—but false—notion that the colorful designs on some Pennsylvania barns are "hex" symbols. The persistent influence of this idea even creeps into the work of professional folklorists, as in Paul Frazier, "Some Lore of Hexing and Powwowing," *Midwest Folklore* 2:2 (Summer 1952), 101-07. Since these signs are associated with German Lutheran and Reformed rather than with Anabaptist and Pietist Pennsylvania-German culture, they are not discussed in this chapter.

8. Lauren Friesen, Goshen, Ind., Aug. 18, 1987 (written text).

9. Larry Lee Chupp, Goshen, Ind., Feb. 11, 1984. Incredibly, Chupp claims that he heard this from a "straitlaced Amish bishop."

10. John A. Hostetler, *Amish Society*, 4th ed. (Baltimore: Johns Hopkins University Press, 1993), 148, 375.

11. *Our Amish Neighbors* (Chicago: University of Chicago Press, 1962), 186.

12. S. L. Yoder, Goshen, Ind., Feb. 21, 1984. Here as elsewhere I am indebted to Yoder's insights into northern Indiana Amish culture, from which he comes. However, it is true that Amish in some districts in the U.S., including Adams and Allen Counties in Indiana, require brief Sunday weddings, following the church service, of couples that are already pregnant. A letter from Adams County printed in the December 1983 issue of the *Budget,* the newspaper that serves Amish worldwide, says that, in 1982, nine of the twenty-five Old Order Amish weddings in Adams County (36%) were for such couples. With more Indiana Amish men being employed full-time away from home during the week, Saturday has gradually become a more customary time for weddings. I am indebted to Steve Nolt, Goshen, Indiana, for this information.

13. *Festival Quarterly* 13:2 (Summer 1986), 38.

14. (Weierhof, 1987), 353. I am indebted to Adalbert Goertz of Waynesboro, Pennsylvania, for this citation.

15. *Festival Quarterly* 11:3 (Fall 1984), 42.

16. Ibid.

17. "A New Look at an Old Problem: Origins of the Variations in Mennonite Plautdietsch," *Mennonite Quarterly Review* 63 (1980), 285-96.

18. S. L. Yoder, Goshen, Ind., Feb. 21, 1984.

19. David Augsburger, Goshen, Ind., Feb. 4, 1983. Assumed in his telling of the story of Menno in the molasses, in chapters 1 and 4. Roelf Kuitse once pastored a Mennonite congregation on the island of Texel, the Netherlands, where this belief is still a living oral tradition. Mennonites have lived there since the sixteenth century. The arrangement is preserved in the Mennonite church, now a museum, at Den Hoorn on the island of Texel. It is also clearly depicted in plates 1 and 2 of *Mennonite Encyclopedia*, vol. 4.

20. John L. Ruth, Bethlehem, Pa., Aug. 4, 1983.

21. Letter from David Luthy, Aylmer, Ont., Aug. 13, 1987.

22. Letter from Ben J. Raber, Baltic, Ohio, to David Luthy, Aylmer, Ont., Oct., 12, 1986.

23. S. L. Yoder, Goshen, Ind., Feb. 21, 1984.

24. Stephen Scott, *The Amish Wedding and Other Special Occasions of the Old Order Communities* (Intercourse, Pa.: Good Books, 1988), 86, 89.

25. C. J. Dyck, Elkhart, Ind., Aug. 4, 1987.

26. "Singing, Hutterite, at Worship," *Mennonite Encyclopedia* 4:532.

27. Cited in Charles Burkhart, "The Church Music of the Old Order

Amish and Old Colony Mennonites," *Mennonite Quarterly Review* 27 (1953), 43. See also Hedwig T. Durnbaugh, "The Amish Singing Style: Theories of Its Origin and Description of Its Singularity," *Pennsylvania Mennonite Heritage* 22:2 (April 1999), 24-31.

28. Joe Springer, Mennonite Historical Library, Goshen, Ind., Oct. 12, 1987.

29. S. L. Yoder, Feb. 21, 1984. When challenged to prove the accuracy of his account, Yoder's Amish informant exclaimed, "It's in the books!" After being asked to name the books, he said, "J. C. Wenger and all those men tell the story." In Yoder's discussion of the legend he offered his own origins belief by repeating several times that the Amish began using hooks and eyes so that they could recognize each other on the streets.

30. *Mennonite Attire through Four Centuries* (Breinigsville, Pa.: Pennsylvania German Society, 1970), 58-59.

31. Mrs. Jacob J. Miller and Mrs. John E. Yoder, *Descendants of Eli V. Yoder and Barbara Eash* (Kalona, Iowa: The Author, 1961), 5.

32. Maggie Glick, Wolcottville, Ind., Oct. 1980 (written version). The nearby village of Emma—predominantly Mennonite and Amish—also has an etiological legend associated with it, whereby the original name of "Eden Mills" was changed to "Emma," the name of the post-mistress, Emma Prough: Harvey S. Frye, *Emma-Town History* (N.p.: The Author, [1984]).

33. Rachel and Kenneth Pellman, *The World of Amish Quilts* (Intercourse, Pa.: Good Books, 1984), 25.

34. (Intercourse, Pa.: Good Books, 1985), 36, 38.

35. Ibid, 39.

36. Ibid, 36.

37. *Early Pennsylvania Arts and Crafts* (New York: A. S. Barnes, 1964), 26.

38. Rebecca Haarer, Shipshewana, Ind., Aug. 6, 1987.

39. Jay Yoder, Goshen, Ind., April 1987.

40. Paton Yoder, "The Structure of the Amish Ministry in the Nineteenth Century," *Mennonite Quarterly Review* 61 (1987), 294, citing *Ein Diener Register von Diener Deaconien und Bischof in Lancaster County und umliegende Gemeinde* (Gordonville, Pa.: Pequea Publishers, 1983), 7.

41. Robert Charles Bishop and Elizabeth Safanda, *A Gallery of Amish Quilts: Design Diversity from a Plain People* (New York: Dutton, 1976), 22-23. See also Barbara Brackman, "The Strip Tradition in European-American Quilts," *The Clarion* 14 (Fall 1989), 44-51.

42. Jan Gleysteen, "The European Roots of Pennsylvania Dutch Art," *Festival Quarterly* (Nov.-Dec. 1980, Jan. 1981), 33.

43. Rachel W. Kreider, "A Yoder Patron Saint?" *Mennonite Life* 23 (1968), 103-05; "The Yoders' St. Theodore," *Mennonite Life* 26 (1971), 155, 165-66.

44. Kreider, "Saint Theodore," 155.

45. A supernatural etiological legend is associated with St. Theodore as patron of bells: "St. Theodore had received a bell as a gift from the Pope at Rome. Since it was so difficult to bring this bell to Sitten, he made an agreement with the Devil for assistance: If Satan would bring the bell and the bishop to Sion before dawn (cockcrow), he would receive the price of a human soul. Thereupon the bishop sat down in the upturned bell and the Devil, in great anticipation, swiftly bore them through the air. But the might of the saint was greater than the cunning of the Devil. At the command of the bishop, the rooster crowed before the Devil had quite completed the journey. St. Theodore then blessed the bell and it rang out far and wide over Rottenbene": Kreider, "St. Theodore," 166.

46. "A very high percentage of Swiss names, and Swiss Mennonite names therefore, are in fact place names": Correspondence from John Oyer, Goshen, Ind., Oct. 23, 1987.

47. Kreider, "Patron Saint," 105.

48. H. S. Bender, "Grebel, Conrad," *Mennonite Encyclopedia* 2:572.

49. J. C. Wenger, Goshen, Ind., June 21, 1981. The Hutterian *Chronicle* records it thus: "These men then spread out a cloak in front of the people, and each one laid his possessions on it with a willing heart—without being forced—so that the needy might be supported in accordance with the teaching of the prophets and apostles.": *The Chronicle of the Hutterian Brethren*, Vol. 1 (Rifton, NY: Plough, 1987), 81.

50. "Jokes and the Discourse on Disaster," *Journal of American Folklore* 100 (1987), 278-79.

51. "Four Functions of Folklore," *Journal of American Folklore* 66 (1953), 344. The Russian Mennonite ethnic slurs, of course, served a different function. In satirizing foolish behavior they applied social pressure in order to maintain "conformity to the accepted patterns of behavior.": Bascom, 346.

Chapter 4: Trickster Tales

1. The main exception is the Netherlands, where, since about 1650, Mennonites have exerted an influence much greater than their numbers would suggest.

2. Paul Schowalter, "Martyrs," *Mennonite Encyclopedia* 3:524. The actual number of Anabaptist martyrs is in dispute. A far smaller number is suggested by Claus-Peter Clasen in his *Anabaptism, A Social*

History, 1525-1618 (Ithaca, N.Y.: Cornell University Press, 1972) and *The Anabaptists in South and Central Germany, Switzerland, and Austria* ([Goshen, Ind.]: Mennonite Historical Society, 1978). However, Clasen's figures do not include Anabaptists from the Lowlands and are based only on those records that happen to have survived. The exact number of Anabaptists executed will never be known.

3. Thieleman Jansz van Braght, trans. Joseph F. Sohm, 7th ed. (Scottdale, Pa.: Mennonite Publishing House, 1964); original ed., *Het Bloedig Tooneel Der Doops-gesinde, En Weereloose Christenen . . .* (Dordrecht, 1660).

4. Most of the American Mennonites discussed here belong to the denomination once known as the (Old) Mennonite Church (of mainly Swiss-Alsatian descent) and are not to be confused with their Amish cousins, the former General Conference Mennonite Church, the Mennonite Brethren Church, or any of the smaller Mennonite groups. The trickster tradition likely varies among these Mennonite groups. For some "Russian" Mennonite trickster stories, see Peter J. Hampton, "My Dad, the Psychologist," *Mennonite Life* 31 (June 1976), 25-27. For some General Conference Mennonite trickster, or "triumph," stories, see James C. Juhnke, "The Victories of Nonresistance: Mennonite Oral Tradition and World War I," *Fides et Historia* 7 (1974), 19-25.

5. John L. Ruth, Goshen, Ind., March 10, 1983.

6. *The Complete Writings of Menno Simons, c. 1496-1561*, trans. Leonard Verduin and ed. J. C. Wenger, with a biography by Harold S. Bender (Scottdale, Pa.: Herald Press, 1956), 521.

7. Christian Neff and H. S. Bender, "Oath," *Mennonite Encyclopedia* 4:4.

8. J. C. Wenger, Goshen, Ind., Jan. 3, 1983.

9. Told by John L. Ruth of Harleysville, Pa., during an evening plenary session at the joint conference of the (Old) Mennonite Church and the General Conference Mennonite Church at Bethelehem, Pa., on Aug. 5, 1983. Unless otherwise noted, all stories in this article are oral texts recorded by the author in informal settings, such as adult Sunday school classes or after-dinner programs in Elkhart County, Ind. Tape recordings have been deposited in the Mennonite Church USA Archives, Goshen, Ind., in the Ervin Beck collection, Hist. MSS 1-306.

10. For a discussion of distinctive Mennonite costume, see Melvin Gingerich, *Mennonite Attire Through Four Centuries* (Breinigsville, Pa.: The Pennsylvania German Society, 1970), particularly the illustration of the plain coat on page 152.

11. Here and in other stories that follow, the humor begins with the Mennonite being called "Father," which indicates that he has been mistaken for a Roman Catholic priest. Since Mennonite ecclesiology is

very Low Church, a minister is never called "Father." Instead, he may be called "Brother" or "Pastor" or, most often, addressed by his given name.

12. Erminie W. Voegelin, "Trickster," *Standard Dictionary of Folklore, Mythology and Legend,* vol. 2, ed. Maria Leach and Jerome Fried (New York: Funk and Wagnalls, 1950), 1124.

13. "Pulpit Humor in Central Pennsylvania," *Pennsylvania Folklife* 19 (1969), 28-36.

14. "Trickster, the Outrageous Hero," in *Our Living Traditions: An Introduction to American Folklore,* ed. Tristram P. Coffin (New York: Basic Books, 1968), 171.

15. *The Trickster: A Study in American Indian Mythology,* 2nd ed. (New York: Schocken Books, 1972), xxiii.

16. Roger D. Abrahams, *Afro-American Folk Tales: Stories from Black Traditions in the New World* (New York: Pantheon Books, 1985), 173.

17. Larry Danielson, "The Dialect Trickster among the Kansas Swedes," *Indiana Folklore* 8 (1975), 39-59.

18. Austin and Alta Fife, *Saints of Sage and Saddle: Folklore among the Mormons* (Salt Lake City: University of Utah Press, 1980), 304-15.

19. William A. Wilson, "Trickster Tales and the Location of Cultural Boundaries: A Mormon Example," *Journal of Folklore Research* 20:1 (1983), 55-66.

20. Abrahams, *Afro-American Folk Tales,* 172.

21. Ed Cray, "The Rabbi Trickster," *Journal of American Folklore* 77 (1964), 331-45.

22. *Frame Analysis* (New York: Harper & Row, 1974), 308-11.

23. J. G. de Hoop Scheffer, "Mennisten-Streken," *Doopsgezinde Bijdragen* (Leeuwarden, 1868), 23-48.

24. Lynn Veach Sadler, *John Bunyan* (Boston: Twayne, 1979), 30.

25. Scheffer, "Mennisten," 23.

26. Ibid, 28.

27. Ibid.

28. Ibid., 29.

29. Ibid., 35-39.

30. The card game was produced in 1978 as a fundraising project by Mennonites in Holland. The cards mentioned here belong to the book, or "quartet," labeled "Doopsgezinde Zegswijzen [Mennonite Proverbial Phrases]." The two other cards in the quartet are "Menniste Hemel [Mennonite heaven]," which depicts a large house on a canal, and "Menniste Susje [Mennonite sister]," which depicts a plant and a young girl. *Menniste Susje* is the popular name for the plant *Saxifraga umberosa* and also refers to the proverbially prudish, somewhat sly young Mennonite woman.

31. A cluster of supernatural legends has also gathered around Menno, some even found in his own writings. Most show his opponents—debaters or pursuers—turning dumb in his presence. They are recorded by Menno's presumed son-in-law, P. J. Twisck, *Chronijck van den Ondergangh der Tyrannen* . . . (Hoorn, 1620), 1067-75. Some have been translated into English as "Providential Deliverances of Menno Simons" by John F. Funk, in *The Complete Works of Menno Simons* (Elkhart, Ind.: J. F. Funk and Brother, 1871), Part 1, 451-52.

32. When informants commented on the story of Menno in the coach, they usually condemned the deception but hastened to add mollifying words on behalf of Menno and the Anabaptist martyrs, in light of their desperate situations. One informant spoke at length about the possibly harmful effect on Mennonite young people of telling them the story of Menno in the coach.

33. A variant in the form of a Moses Dissinger story appears in Richard Dorson, *American Folklore* (Chicago: University of Chicago Press, 1959), 84.

34. Katie Funk Wiebe, "Mennonite Innocents Abroad," *Festival Quarterly* (Nov. 1979), 34. For more about David Joris as deceiver, see Gary K. Waite, "Staying Alive: The Methods of Survival as Practiced by an Anabaptist Fugitive," *Mennonite Quarterly Review* 61 (Jan. 1987), 46-57.

Chapter 5: The Reggie Jackson Urban Legend

1. The story appeared in the *Cincinnati Enquirer* on January 4, 1982 and the *Phoenix* (Arizona) *Magazine* in September 1982, as well as in many other publications between those dates. I am grateful to Jan Brunvand of the University of Utah for supplying some of the newspaper references cited in this chapter.

2. *Encyclopedia of Urban Legends* (Denver: ABC Clio, 2001), 131.

3. Jan Brunvand, *The Study of American Folklore: An Introduction*, 4th ed. (New York: Norton, 1998), 205.

4. For discussions of these legends, see *The Encyclopedia of Urban Legends*, as well as the many preceding books on urban legends by Brunvand.

5. Jan Brunvand, *The Choking Doberman* (New York: Norton, 1984).

6. William A. Wilson, "'The Vanishing Hitchhiker' among the Mormons," *Indiana Folklore* 8 (1975), 79-97.

7. The tape recordings, transcriptions, and notes for this and all other full and partial texts in this chapter have been deposited in the archives of the Mennonite Church USA, 1700 S. Main, Goshen, Ind., in the Ervin Beck Collection, Hist. MSS 1-306.

8. The ads appeared on June 30, July 7, July 14 and July 21. The

text of the first one read: "Esther Diener Announces a / 'Reggie / Jackson' / Special/ at / Das Essen Haus / Pettisville / Watch the paper for further details / and announcement." The final one said: " . . . Hog Roast . . . Served under a tent, south side of Das / Essen Haus Restaurant. In case of rain, hog / roast dinners will be served in the Attic. / Live Entertainment / Complete Meal . . ." The Essen Haus seems to be a place where urban legends settle in that community. One of my texts of the urban legend of the keys in the stolen handbag is also set at that restaurant.

9. Wilson, "Vanishing Hitchhiker."

10. One exception is that in the 1990s a version of the vanishing hitchhiker urban legend circulated among Mennonites in Lancaster County, Pennsylvania. That legend often surfaces during revival meetings or "spiritual emphasis" weeks.

11. All of these legends are discussed in Brunvand's *Encyclopedia of Urban Legends*. The story of the disappearing Amish grandmother was presumably printed in *The Budget*, the newspaper that serves the international Amish community.

12. "The Kentucky Fried Rat: Legends and Modern Society," *Journal of the Folklore Institute* 17 (1980), 222-43.

13. J. Howard Kauffman and Leland J. Harder, *Anabaptists Four Centuries Later* (Scottdale, Pa.: Herald Press, 1975), 283-84.

14. Willard H. Smith, *Mennonites in Illinois* (Scottdale, Pa.: Herald Press, 1983), 262-80.

15. In thus recasting the story, he shapes it according to many American versions in which the people in the elevators are three couples rather than three women. See, for instance, the versions in the *Detroit Free Press*, Feb. 25, 1982, and the *Akron Beacon Journal*, July 14, 1982. The Mennonite versions in my collection are always about three women alone in the elevator.

16. In the *Phoenix* version, for instance, "The ladies were in their eighties."

17. For a discussion of distinctive Mennonite costume, see Melvin Gingerich, *Mennonite Attire Through Four Centuries* (Breinigsville, Pa.: The Pennsylvania German Society, 1970), particularly the illustrations on pp. 117 and 152.

18. The telling of the legend elicited a more elaborate, impromptu acting out at a large family reunion in Archbold, Ohio, in the summer of 1982. The teller, who had commanded the attention of all present, suddenly called on people in the audience who knew the legend to join him by acting out the roles of the frightened women, Reggie Jackson, and the dog.

19. Richard Kauffman, "Letters," Aug. 23, 1982, 6.

20. In a storytelling session by John L. Ruth at "Bethlehem '83," Aug. 6, 1983.

21. For a discussion of the doctrine see Harold S. Bender, et al., "Nonconformity," *Mennonite Encyclopedia* 3:890-97; also J. C. Wenger, *Separated unto God* (Scottdale, Pa.: Herald Press, 1955).

22. This stereotypical notion is false, however, according to some Mennonites from eastern Pennsylvania, who say that interest in professional baseball is so ingrained among Mennonites there that older women would indeed know who Reggie Jackson is.

23. As in the version that appeared in the *Akron Beacon Journal*.

24. Kauffman and Harder, *Anabaptists Four Centuries Later*, 136-41.

25. "Introduction" to J. Daniel Hess, *Integrity: Let Your Yea Be Yea* (Scottdale, Pa.: Herald Press, 1978), 9.

26. "A Christian Living Forum," *Christian Living* 28 (Dec. 1981), 14-20.

27. Conversation, Goshen, Ind., Aug. 10, 1983.

28. To some extent, the same is probably true for the Quakers and the Brethren—two groups who have also, historically, refused to swear an oath. For some comments on Quaker attitudes, see Richard Bauman, "Quaker Folk Linguistics and Folklore," in *Folklore: Performance and Communication*, ed. Dan Ben-Amos and Kenneth Goldstein (The Hague: Mouton, 1975), 257. Apparently the only study of Brethren narratives is concerned with "true" personal-experience stories. See Rebecca Ziegler, "'Strangers and Exiles': Narratives from the Brethren," *Folklore and Mythology Studies* 1 (1977), 23-36.

29. Melissa Miller and Phil M. Shenk (Scottdale, Pa.: Herald Press, 1982).

30. For some World War I martyrs' stories from oral circulation, however, see James C. Juhnke, "The Victories of Nonresistance: Mennonite Oral Tradition and World War I," *Fides et Historia* 7 (1974), 19-25.

31. Terms used by Brunvand in *Study of American Folklore*, 113-14.

Chapter 6: CPS Protest Songs

1. Robert S. Kreider, "The 'Good Boys' of CPS," *Mennonite Life* (Sept. 1991), 4. See also Albert N. Keim, *The CPS Story: An Illustrated History of Civilian Public Service* (Intercourse, Pa.: Good Books, 1990); Perry Bush, *Two Kingdoms, Two Loyalties: Mennonite Pacifism in Modern America* (Baltimore: Johns Hopkins University Press, 1998); and Melvin Gingerich, *Service for Peace: A History of Mennonite Civilian Public Service* (Akron, Pa.: Mennonite Central Committee, 1949). One of the self-described "bad boys" of CPS was William Stafford, of Church of the Brethren background, who became a distinguished American poet. See his memoir, *Down in My Heart: Peace Witness in Wartime* (Corvallis: Oregon State University Press, 1998) and an anthology of his pacifist writings edited by his son Kim:

Every War Has Two Losers: William Stafford on Peace and War (N.P.: Milkweed Editions, 2003).

2. Quoted in Perry Bush, "We Have Learned to Question Government," *Mennonite Life* (June 1990), 14.

3. John Greenway regards this song as "unquestionably the greatest song yet produced by American labor": *American Folksongs of Protest* (Philadelphia: University of Pennsylvania Press, 1953), 181. The tune to which it is sung is used in many other labor protest songs.

4. "Colonel" may refer to Col. Lewis F. Kosch, assistant to Lewis B. Hershey. It probably does not refer to Hershey himself, since he was usually referred to as "General Hershey."

5. Greenway, "Introduction," *American Folksongs of Protest*, 1-19.

6. R. S. McCarl, "Occupational Folklore," in *American Folklore: An Encyclopedia*, ed. Jan Brunvand (New York: Garland, 1996), 521.

Chapter 7: Painting on Glass
1. Ervin Beck, "Mennonite and Amish Painting on Glass," *Mennonite Quarterly Review* 63:2 (1989), 115-49.

Chapter 8: Indiana Amish Family Records
1. David Luthy, "One Hundred Years of Amish Genealogies, 1885-1985," *Pennsylvania Mennonite Heritage* 8 (Oct. 1985), 28-30.

2. John A. Hostetler, *Amish Society*, 4th ed. (Baltimore: Johns Hopkins University Press, 1993), 244.

3. Ibid., 245.

Chapter 9: The Relief Sale Festival
1. "The Place of Festival in the Worldview of the Seventeenth-Century Quakers," in *Time Out of Time: Essays on the Festival*, ed. Alessandro Falassi (Albuquerque: University of New Mexico Press, 1987), 98.

2. Quotations by relief sale participants come from field observation reports completed by students in my folklore classes at Goshen College in 1982, 1984, and 1999. "The 1999 Michiana Mennonite Relief Sale as Folk Festival," a loose-leaf notebook surveying eight different aspects of the sale, has been deposited in the Mennonite Historical Library at Goshen College. The manila folder, "Relief Sale Field Observations," has been deposited in the Mennonite Church USA Archives, Goshen, Indiana. I am indebted to my former students for these materials.

3. The relationship between the relief sale and folk festival has been noted in several other sources, although not explored in detail: Robert S. Kreider and Rachel Waltner Goossen, "Organizing Festivals for

MCC: Relief Sales" in their *Hungry, Thirsty, a Stranger: The MCC Experience* (Scottdale, Pa.: Herald Press, 1988), 361-69; Griselda Shelly, "Relief Sales," *Mennonite Encyclopedia* 5:759-60; Erin Roth, "Relief Sales in the Midwest," in *Encyclopedia of Midwestern Folklore* (forthcoming).

4. Beverly J. Stoeltje, "Festival," in *International Encyclopedia of Communications*, vol. 2, ed. Erik Barnouw (New York: Oxford University Press, c. 1989), 161.

5. Marianne Mesnil, "Place and Time in the Carnivalesque Festival," in *Time Out of Time: Essays on the Festival*, ed. Alessandro Falassi (Albuquerque: University of New Mexico Press, 1987), 186.

6. Stoeltje, "Festival," 161.

7. Alessandro Falassi, "Festival: Definition and Morphology," in *Time Out of Time*, 3.

8. Ibid.

9. Mesnil, "Place and Time," in Falassi, *Time Out of Time*, 192.

10. Falassi, "Festival" in Ibid, 3.

11. This is the anthem version of the doxology, "Praise God from Whom All Blessings Flow," using a tune published in 1830 by the Boston Handel and Haydn Society. The song first appeared in *The Mennonite Hymnal* published in 1969 (Scottdale, Pa.: Herald Press), where it was number 606. The hymn became a favorite, especially for large Mennonite assemblies, and has continued to be called, affectionately, "606," even though it now appears as number 118 in *The Hymnal: A Worship Book* (Scottdale, Pa.: Mennonite Publishing House), which replaced *The Mennonite Hymnal* in 1992. Many Mennonites sing this difficult hymn from memory.

12. Ibid, 4.

13. Ibid, 4.

14. Ibid, 5.

15. Conversation with director of the Elkhart County Visitors Bureau, Bristol, Ind., April 25, 2002.

16. Falassi, "Festival" in *Time Out of Time*, 5.

17. Victor Turner, "Humility and Hierarchy: The Liminality of Status Elevation and Reversal" in his *The Ritual Process: Structure and Anti-Structure* (Ithaca, N.Y.: Cornell University Press, 1969), 166-203.

18. In years when men build a house and it is sold, with all proceeds going to the sale, the contribution of men's work to the sale is greater, since the houses sell for well over $100,000.

19. Rachel Waltner Goossen and Robert S. Kreider cite one vociferous critic of relief sales who has never attended a sale: "Organizing Festivals for MCC: Relief Sales," 367.

20. Chapter 5, "Humility and Hierarchy: The Liminality of Status Elevation and Reversal," in Turner, *The Ritual Process*, 166-203.

21. Mikhail Bakhtin, *Rabelais and His World*, trans. Helene Iswolsky (Cambridge, Mass.: MIT Press, 1968).

22. The fourth weekend in September, which is the annual date of the Michiana Relief Sale, always falls near September 29, which is the festival of St. Michael, or Michaelmas, in the traditional church year. The Amish of Lancaster County observe Michaelmas as a holiday for rest and fasting prior to a communion service. When Amish and Mennonites lived in Europe, Michaelmas was the day when rents were due, following harvest, and was also an occasion for giving some of one's wealth to the poor. I am indebted for these insights to Julia Kasdorf, e-mail correspondence, Sept. 30, 2002.

23. Interview, Goshen, Ind., July, 2002.

24. In her *Mennonite Encyclopedia 5* article, Griselda Shelley cites the objections to relief sales as being "commercialism and undercutting voluntary giving" and the fact that they do "little to promote a responsible Christian lifestyle" (760).

25. John Bender, "Down-Home Hospitality Pervades Mennonite Relief Sale," *South Bend Tribune* ["Michiana" magazine section] Sept. 16, 1979, pp. 10-13.

26. There are at least three ways to rationalize the eating of food at the sale in order to feed the hungry elsewhere. First, "grazing" from one food booth to the other may be a more typical consumption pattern than actual over-indulgence. Second, if one divides proceeds from food booths by the number of persons in attendance, the consumption per person is reasonable, especially since sale-goers also purchase food to eat at home. Finally, people in the food-deprived cultures to which MCC relief aid goes are likely to celebrate with feasting when food is abundant, rather than save it for times of scarcity. The issue has become somewhat defused since MCC now emphasizes general assistance rather than hunger relief—"helping" rather than "feeding."

27. For this and information on MCC's role in promoting relief sales in the U.S. and Canada, I am indebted to a telephone conversation with Douglas Berg on August 27, 2002. After I read a paper on this topic at the conference on Mennonite ritual at Hillsdale (MI) College in June 2003, Kerry Strayer reported that, after one location experienced a sudden decline one year in sales revenue, the leaders checked and found that the sale had occurred on a Jewish holy day. Since then, they have made sure that there is no conflict of the sale date with Jewish events. Strayer did not remember which sale the story refers to. Although it might be a "true" story, the narrative has been detached from its location and has therefore become a folk legend. Along with the relief sale proverbs and the anecdote about "Run for Relief," cited above, this legend shows that the sale as a calendric custom is clearly generating its own folklore in various genres. I would like to receive additional examples.

28. Julia Kasdorf, "Bakhtin, Boundaries and Bodies," *Mennonite Quarterly Review* 71.2 (April 1997), 169-88; Rudy Wiebe, "The Body Knows as Much as the Soul: On the Human Reality of Being a Writer," *Mennonite Quarterly Review* 71.2 (April 1997), 189-200; Beth Martin Birky, "When Flesh Becomes Word: Creating Space for the Female Body in Mennonite Women's Poetry," *Mennonite Quarterly Review* 72.4 (Oct. 1998), 677-88; Pamela Classen, "What's Bre(a)d in the Bone: The Bodily Heritage of Mennonite Women," *Mennonite Quarterly Review* 68.2 (April 1994), 229-47.

29. "Quilts, Zweibach and Oak Furniture: Mennonite Material Culture as Material Aid," unpublished paper presented at the meeting of the American Folklore Society, Anchorage, Alaska, Oct. 20, 2001.

30. Richard Bauman, "The Place of Festival in the Worldview of the Seventeenth-Century Quakers," in Falassi, *Time Out of Time*, 95; Stoeltje, "Festival," 161; Roger D. Abrahams, "An American Vocabulary of Celebrations," in Falassi, *Time Out of Time*, 174-77.

Suggested Readings

This list of sources for additional reading surveys the broader scope of Mennonite folklore studies, ranging into various Mennonite groups, geographic locales and types of folklore. For a more exhaustive list, see website: www.goshen.edu/~ervinb/links.html.

Abrahams, Ethel. *Frakturmalen und Schoenschreiben.* North Newton, Kan.: The Author, 1980.

Amsler, Cory M., ed. *Bucks County Fraktur.* Doylestown, Pa.: Bucks County Historical Society, 2001.

Arthur, Linda Boynton. "Clothing is a Window to the Soul: The Social Control of Women in a Holdeman Mennonite Community. *Journal of Mennonite Studies* 15 (1997), 11-30.

Beck, Ervin. "Mennonite and Amish Painting on Glass." *Mennonite Quarterly Review* 63 (April 1989), 115-49.

———. "Plain and Fancy: A Review of Research in Mennonite Folk Arts." *Mennonite Quarterly Review* 71:1 (Jan. 1997), 69-91.

Bird, Michael S. *Ontario Fraktur: A Pennsylvania German Folk Art Tradition in Early Canada.* Toronto: M. F. Feheley, 1977.

Brednich, Rolf. *Mennonite Folklife and Folklore: A Preliminary Report.* Ottawa: National Museums of Canada, 1977.

Bronner, Simon. "'We Live What I Paint and I Paint What I See: A Mennonite Artist in Northern Indiana." *Indiana Folklore* 12 (1979), 5-17.

Burke, Susan M., and Matthew H. Hill, eds. *From Pennsylvania to Waterloo: Pennsylvania-German Folk Culture in Transition.* Kitchener, Ont.: Friends of the Joseph Schneider Haus, 1991.

[Church architecture special issue.] *Mennonite Quarterly Review* 73:2 (April 1999).

Doerksen, Victor G. "The Anabaptist Martyr Ballad." *Mennonite Quarterly Review* 51 (Jan. 1977), 5-21.

Dow, James. "Chiasmus, Structural Symmetry, and Nonverbal Communication: Toward an Understanding of the Old Order Amish Gemee." *Zeitschrift fur Dialektologie und Linguistik* 64 (1989), 125-36.

Durnbaugh, Hedwig T. "The Amish Singing Style: Theories of Its Origin and Description of Its Singularity." *Pennsylvania Mennonite Heritage* 22:2 (April 1999), 24-31.

Enninger, Werner. "Amish By-Names." *Names* (Dec. 1985), 243-58.

———. *Bibliographie Enninger.* Essen, Germany: The Author, 1988. *A guide to many studies of Anabaptist dialects in North America.*

Ensminger, Robert F. *The Pennsylvania Barn: Its Origin, Evolution and Distribution in North America.* Baltimore: Johns Hopkins University Press, 1992.

Fabian, Monroe. "Sulfur Inlay in Pennsylvania German Furniture." *Pennsylvania Folklife* (Fall 1977), 2-9.

Friesen, Rudy P., and Sergey Shmakin. *Into the Past: Buildings of the Mennonite Commonwealth.* Winnipeg: Roduga, 1996.

Friesen, Steve. "Emil 'Maler' Kym, Great Plains Folk Artist." *The Clarion* (Fall 1978), 34-39.

Friesen, Victor Carl. *The Windmill Turning: Nursery Rhymes, Maxims, and Other Expressions of Western Canadian Mennonites.* Edmonton: University of Alberta, 1988.

Gehret, Ellen J. *This Is the Way I Pass My Time.* Birdsboro, Pa.: Pennsylvania German Society, 1985. *On decorated towels.*

Gingerich, Melvin. *Mennonite Attire Through Four Centuries.* Breinigsville, Pa.: Pennsylvania German Society, 1970.

Godshall, Jeffrey L. "The Traditional Farmhouse of the Franconia Mennonite Community." *Pennsylvania Mennonite Heritage* (Jan. 1983), 22-25.

Granick, Eve Wheatcroft. *The Amish Quilt.* Intercourse, Pa.: Good Books, 1989.

Herr, Patricia. *Amish Arts of Lancaster County.* Atglen, Pa.: Schiffer, 1998.

Hersh, Tandy. *Samplers of the Pennsylvania Germans.* Kutztown, Pa.: Pennsylvania German Society, 1991.

Hess, Clarke E. *Mennonite Arts.* Atglen, Pa.: Schiffer, 2001.

Hostetler, John A. "The Amish Use of Symbols and Their Function in Bounding the Community." *The Journal of the Royal Anthropological Institute* 94:1 (1963), 11-22.

———. "Folk and Scientific Medicine in Amish Society." *Human Organization* (Winter 1963-64), 269-75.

Hughes, Robert. *Amish: The Art of the Quilt.* New York: Knopf, 1990.

Janzen, John, and Reinhild Kauenhoven Janzen. *Mennonite Furniture: A Migrant Tradition (1766-1910).* Intercourse, Pa.: Good Books, 1991.

Janzen, Reinhild Kauenhoven. "Keeping Faith and Keeping Time: Old Testament Images on Mennonite Clocks." *Mennonite Life* 55:4 (Dec. 2000). *On-line publication.*

Kaufman, Stanley. *Heatwole and Suter Pottery.* Harrisonburg, Va.: Eastern Mennonite College, 1978.

——— and Leroy Beachy. *Amish in Eastern Ohio.* Walnut Creek, Ohio: German Culture Museum, 1990.

——— and Ricky Clark. *Germanic Folk Culture in Eastern Ohio.* Walnut Creek, Ohio: German Culture Museum, 1986.

Klassen, Doreen. *Singing Mennonite: Low German Songs among the Mennonites.* Winnipeg: University of Manitoba Press, 1988.

Locher, Paul G., et al. *Decorative Arts of Ohio's Sonnenberg Mennonites.* Kidron, Ohio: Kidron Community Historical Society, 1994.

Luthy, David. *Amish Folk Artist Barbara Ebersol: Her Life, Fraktur, and Death Record Book.* Lancaster, Pa.: Lancaster Mennonite Historical Society, 1995.

McCabe-Juhnke, John. "Enacting Gemeinde in the Language and Style of Swiss Volhynian Mennonite Storytelling." *Heritage of the Great Plains* 27:2 (Summer 1994), 21-38.

McCauley, Daniel and Kathryn McCauley. *Decorative Arts of the Amish of Lancaster County.* Intercourse, Pa.: Good Books, 1988.

McKegney, Patricia P. *Charm for Me, Mr. Eby: Folk Medicine in Southern Ontario, 1890-1920.* Wellesley, Ont.: Bamberg Press, 1989.

McLary, Kathleen. *Amish Style: Clothing, Home Furnishings, Toys, Dolls and Quilts.* Bloomington: Indiana University Press, 1993.

Miller, Harry H. "The Sleeping Preachers: An Historical Study of the Role of Charisma in Amish Society." *Pennsylvania Folklife* 18 (Winter 1968-69), 19-31.

Miller, Levi. "The Role of a Braucher-Chiropractor in an Amish Community." *Mennonite Quarterly Review* 55 (April 1981), 157-71.

Muller, Charles M. *Soap Hollow: The Furniture and Its Makers.* Groveport, Ohio: Canal Press, 2002.

Nykor, Lynda M. and Patricia D. Musson. *Mennonite Furniture: The Ontario Tradition in York County.* Toronto: J. Lorimer, 1977.

Patterson, Nancy-Lou. "Death and Ethnicity: Swiss-German Mennonite Gravestones of the 'Pennsylvania Style' (1804-54) in the Waterloo Region, Ontario." *Mennonite Life* (Sept. 1982), 4-7.

———. "'I See the Vernal Landscape Glowing': The Symbolic Landscape of the Swiss-German Mennonite Settlers in Waterloo County." *Mennonite Life* (Dec. 1983), 8-16.

———. *Swiss-German and Dutch-German Mennonite Traditional Arts in the Waterloo Region, Ontario.* Ottawa: National Museums of Canada, 1979.

Pellman, Rachel, and Kenneth. *A Treasury of Mennonite Quilts.* Intercourse, Pa.: Good Books, 1992.

Rechlin, Alice T. M. "The Utilization of Space by the Nappanee, Indiana, Old Order Amish: A Minority Group Study." *Mennonite Quarterly Review* 46 (Jan. 1972), 84-85.

Reimer, Al, et al., eds. *A Sackful of Plautdietsch: A Collection of Mennonite Low German Stories and Poems.* Winnipeg: Hyperion Press, 1983.

Schlabach, Kyle. *The Cow in Science Hall and Other Goshen College Folklore.* Goshen, Ind.: Pinchpenny Press, 1994.

Scott, Stephen. *Amish Houses and Barns.* Intercourse, Pa.: Good Books, 1992.

———. *The Amish Wedding and Other Special Occasions of Old Order Communities.* Intercourse, Pa.: Good Books, 1988.

———. *Plain Buggies: Amish, Mennonite and Brethren Horse-Drawn Transportation.* Intercourse, Pa.: Good Books, 1981.

Thompson, Chad L. "Yodeling of the Indiana Swiss Amish." *Anthropological Linguistics* (Fall 1996), 495-520.

Weaver, Laura. "When the Strings Go, Everything Goes: The Metamorphosis of a Mennonite Cap." *Mississipi Folklore Register* 21 (Spring-Fall 1987), 41-54.

Webster, Donald B. *The William Eby Pottery, Conestogo, Ontario, 1855-1907.* Toronto: Royal Ontario Museum, 1971.

Wood, Stacy B. *Clockmakers and Watchmakers of Lancaster County, Pennsylvania.* Lancaster, Pa.: Lancaster County Historical Society, 1995.

Yoder, Don. "Fraktur in Mennonite Culture." *Mennonite Quarterly Review* 48 (July 1974), 35-42.

Yoder-Sickler, Telissa, ed. *J. C. Penney and Other Camp Skits.* Goshen, Ind.: Pinchpenny Press, 1994.

Credits

The author has obtained permission from the following publications to reprint the essays, in revised form, as chapters in *MennoFolk*:
"Stories and Functions," was first published as "Stories Mennonites Tell," *Gospel Herald*, Jan. 31, 1984.

"Origin Tales and Beliefs" was first published as "Mennonite and Amish Origin Tales and Beliefs," *Mennonite Quarterly Review* 64 (Jan. 1990).

"Trickster Tales" was first published as "Mennonite Trickster Tales: True to be Good," *Mennonite Quarterly Review* 61 (Jan. 1987).

"The Reggie Jackson Urban Legend" was first published as "Reggie Jackson among the Mennonites," *Mennonite Quarterly Review* 58 (April 1984).

"CPS Protest Songs," was first published as "CPS Protest Songs," *Mennonite Life* (Dec. 1996).

"Painting on Glass," was first published as "Glass Painting by Plain People" in *Folklife Annual*, ed. James Hardin and Alan Jabbour (Washington, D.C.: American Folklife Center, 1988).

"Indiana Amish Family Records," was first published as "Indiana Amish Family Records," *Pennsylvania Folklife* (Winter 1989-90). Reprinted with permission of the Pennsylvania Folklife Society, Ursinus College, Collegeville, PA 19426.

"The Relief Sale Festival" was commissioned for *The Measure of My Days*, ed. Joe Miller and Reuben Miller (Telford, Pa.: Cascadia, 2004). Copyright © 2004 by Cascadia Publishing House. Used by permission, all rights reserved.

Photos in chapters 1 and 2 are used with permission of Goshen College, Public Relations Historical Photographs, and courtesy of the Mennonite Church USA Archives, Goshen, Ind.

Photo of Amish quilt in chapter 3 is used with permission of the United States Postal Service.

Photo of J. C. Wenger in chapter 4 is used with permission of the Mennonite Historical Library, Goshen, Ind. Images of the Dutch playing cards are used courtesy of the Mennonite Historical Library, Goshen, Ind.

Photo of Esther Diener in chapter 5 is used with the permission of Ervin Beck.

Photos in chapter 6 are used with permission of Mary Beck.

Photos in chapter 7 taken by and used with permission of Jeff Hochstedler. They appear here courtesy of the Mennonite Church USA Archives, Goshen, Ind.

Photo of Jewel Ann Miller birth record, wedding favors, and Howard Nisley family record in chapter 8 taken by and used with permission of Ervin Beck. All other photos in chapter 8 taken by and used with permission of Jeff Hochstedler.

Photos in chapter 9 are used courtesy of the Mennonite Historical Library, Goshen, Ind. Photo on page 192 taken by Chris Kennel and Andre King, page 195 by Anne Horst and Deborah Scott, page 199 by Michael Yoder and Nathan Kraft. All are used with permission.

The Author

Ervin Beck was Professor of English at Goshen College from 1967 to 2003, teaching English, folklore, and postcolonial and Mennonite literature. He has also been a visiting scholar at the University of Sheffield and the University of Warwick, in England, and Fulbright Professor of English at University College of Belize. He has published widely in scholarly journals on folklore, folk arts, English literature, postcolonial literature and Mennonite studies.